WHAT THE WORLD NEEDS NOW

A Resource Book for Daydreamers,
Frustrated Inventors, Cranks,
Efficiency Experts, Utopians,
Gadgeteers, Tinkerers and
Just About Everybody Else
(Third Edition)

Written and Illustrated by
STEVEN M. JOHNSON

With a Foreword by
ROGER von OECH, PH.D
Author of A WHACK ON THE SIDE OF THE HEAD

PATENT DEPENDING PRESS
www.patentdepending.com

Also by Steven M. Johnson
Public Therapy Buses, Information Specialty Bums, Solar Cook-A-Mats and Other Visions of the 21st Century

First edition: Ten Speed Press, 1984
Second edition: Ten Speed Press, 2001
Third edition: Patent Depending Press, 2012

Patent Depending Press
www.patentdepending.com
Torrance, California

ISBN-13: 978-0615630410
ISBN-10: 0615630413
LCCN: 2012906811

Third Edition: May 2012

Printed in the United States of America

ACKNOWLEDGEMENTS

Since this is a first book, it is an opportunity to acknowledge publicly the guidance and encouragement of a handful of people who have helped me in past years. Of course, these persons are neither to be blamed nor credited for my eccentricities, nor for my frustrated attempts to become an inventor of marginally useful things.

Looking at the Acknowledgments page that appeared in the first edition of this book, I see that all of the mentors whom I thanked and praised are deceased. They remain often in my thoughts: my mother, Eugenie B. Johnson, editor and librarian; my father, Paul C. Johnson, for many years Editor-in-Chief of Sunset Books and author of several Western pictorial books; Josef Albers, Bauhaus founder who taught drawing classes at Yale University during the years I was an undergraduate there; William K. Bronson, author and magazine editor; Roger Olmsted, author and magazine editor; Allan Temko, architecture critic and columnist for *The San Francisco Chronicle*, author, and teacher; and Art Hoppe, author and nationally-syndicated columnist for *The San Francisco Chronicle*.

Looking back to the First Edition, I once again acknowledge Ten Speed Press Editorial Director George Young, who was uncommonly helpful and gentle in guiding this book to completion.

Daily companions, critics and helpmates are my wife Beatrice, student of Sanskrit and Vedanta philosophy and religion, and community college instructor; and my son Alex, author and university professor.

Steven M. Johnson, 2012

FOREWORD

Take a look around. I'll bet there are a few things you'd like to change. That's just what Steve Johnson thought. For example:

❑ Tired of your favorite shoes wearing out just when they were getting to be comfortable? Then get the "10-Year Shoe" that rolls up on itself (see page 2). Ingenious!
❑ Would you like to eat with your fingers, but are afraid that you don't have the proper utensils? Your prayers have been answered with "Silver Wear." (See page 45.)
❑ How about an umbrella that combines dual-utility and fashion? You've got a number of choices with the "Tiebrella," the"Umbrella Hat," and the "Umbrella Holster." (See page 24.)
❑ And then there are the "Exercuisine" (an exercise-powered food processor), "Toilets for Two," and the "Yogamobile" (80 pure thoughts to the mile).

These are just some of the inventions that will whet your imagination. Steve allows us in dramatic fashion one of the key principles of creative thinking: new ideas come from connecting previously unconnected ideas. In the same way that Gutenberg combined the wine press and the coin punch to create movable type and the printing press, Steve shows us how to combine a bed and a desk to create the "Nod Office."

How practical are these ideas? Well, you be the judge. Or better yet, don't judge them at all. I think the real value of the concepts presented here is that they are "stepping stones," that is, ideas that may not be practical in their own right, but that may lead our thinking in new directions.

As I see it, creative thinking is an outlook, an attitude, a way of asking "what if?" and "why not?" However, much of what prevents us from exercising this outlook is that we become prisoners of familiarity. The more we see or do something in the same way, the more difficult it is to think about doing it any other way. Thus we need a good jolting of our mental apparatus—I call it "a whack on the side of the head"—to allow us to see other possibilities. This book is a good jolt. It forces us to suspend our everyday assumptions about what we think is real and possible. For example, most of us assume that we don't eat with eyeglasses. But if we ask, "What if we could?" we come up with the "Goggles Dining Kit." How obvious could anything be!

Also, this book highlights one other principle of creative thinking: it's a lot of fun. Think of this as Steve's invitation to use your imagination and make up your own ideas. Good luck!

Roger van Oech
President,
Creative Think,
and author of
A Whack on the Side of the Head

PREFACE TO THE THIRD EDITION

What The World Needs Now has had an interesting history since it was first published in 1984. The book appeared long before the Internet, Web pages or small personal cell phones were in common use. My silly concepts were nothing more than an attempt to spin out ideas for possible "what if?" products. I was amused by my plan to mimic glossy product catalogs, and to introduce a line of products that didn't exist.

I was not trying to predict anything, but amazingly many of these concepts were later marketed as serious products by reputable manufacturers. Not long after the book appeared in bookstores, one could purchase a small, bear-shaped rucksack (page 88), cuddly animal-shaped sleeping bags for children (page 103), or water-filled barbells for busy travelers (page 36). Multi-use furnishings like my flip-over desk concepts (pages 62-63) came on the market. My radically inappropriate business wear styles for men and women (pages 16-17) anticipated actual styles that mixed and matched apparel categories so promiscuously that 28 years later, my styles look old-fashioned.

BOW TIE GLASSES CASE

The book generated radio interviews where newscasters interspersed traffic reports with attempts to extract the "meaning" of my book by having me describe my concepts haltingly over the phone. As a guest of a local Sacramento TV show I was treated politely but as if I had arrived from a different planet. The purpose of these interviews was to poke fun at me, and the interviewers had a big laugh over my ridiculous concepts.

A representative for *The Tonight Show* saw the book and phoned me in late 1987 asking if any of my products were "made." I said no but I would gladly make some. From November to December I commissioned the world's first info-toilet (page 75) to be built, and hired a seamstress to sew a wearable bow tie with a zipper that held a pair of reading glasses (page 41) and to tailor a man's sport

TOILETS FOR THE STUDIOUS

Author modeling an Info-Toilet and Bow Tie Glasses Case, 1987.

SLIPPERSHINES

LIGHTSHOES ASSURE THAT YOUR HANDS ARE FREE WHILE NEGOTIATING HALLWAYS OR BACKWOODS TRAILS AT NIGHT. MOST SOPHISTICATED IS THE *SLIPPERSHINE* SERIES. *SLIPPERSHINES* ARE PARKED AT ALL TIMES IN A RE-CHARGING STATION. ILLUMINATED HEEL LOCATORS, L AND H, ARE PRESSURE-SENSITIVE LIGHTSWITCHES.

PLUG-INS

PLUG-INS OFFER FEWER FEATURES THAN *SLIPPER-SHINES*, BUT REQUIRE LESS APPARATUS. THE SHOES, WITH NIGHTLIGHT, SIMPLY PLUG INTO ANY SOCKET TO RECHARGE THE NI-CAD BATTERIES.

A pair of double-decker Slippershines that were demonstrated on *The Tonight Show* in December 1987.

The aging author.

coat that included a hidden daypack (page 21). I made a pair of Slippershines myself, sewing together a pair two-story slippers that included a working flashlight in the upper story with concealed wiring connected to an operable switch at the side of each slipper (page 28). Ed McMahon and Johnny Carson demonstrated the slippers on the "Christmas Products Show" that December.

In 1989, Ten Speed Press publisher Phil Wood expressed frustration that my book was not selling well enough in bookstores alongside *The Far Side* and *Garfield* humor books, and paid for a booth at The Invention Convention in Pasadena, California to promote *What The World Needs Now*. The booth was decorated with large prints of my concepts, including an image of Cigaire, a smoking helmet (page 35). In another booth, a nearly identical product was demonstrated by an elderly inventor who said his friend had died from exposure to secondhand smoke. Great minds think alike.

CIGAIRE

SMOKE-HOODS WITH SMOKE-LESS ASHTRAYS, IN SEVERAL STYLES.

MEN'S:
EQUALLY APPROPRIATE "DOWNTOWN" OR AT THE CONSTRUCTION SITE OFFICE.

WOMEN'S:
GLOSS BLACK ENAMEL, BRUSHED ALUMINUM AND WASHABLE FLOPPY BRIM.

Though *What The World Needs Now* is clearly out-of-date with respect to technology and social trends–CRT tube radiation (page 53) and smoking at the office are no longer topics of public concern–it continues to attract readers who enjoy thinking about the possibility that they, too, might invent something peculiar or even useful. Five years ago I learned from talented California-based industrial designer Dirk Dieter, *www.verb2. com*, that *What The World Needs Now* had been passed around among industrial designers. Wow! What, I wondered, could they have possibly learned from me? But I accepted the information as a cherished endorsement.

Steven M. Johnson, 2012

– CONTENTS –

CLOTHING. 1

PERSONAL EQUIPMENT 23

DINING TECHNOLOGY. 43

OFFICE FURNISHINGS AND SUPPLIES. 51

HOME FURNISHINGS AND APPLIANCES. 61

GARDENING GADGETS 81

CAMPING AND SURVIVAL GEAR. 87

TRANSPORTATION. 117

AUTHOR'S TIPS FOR INVENTING THINGS 149

CLOTHING

MONEY-SAVING DOUBLE-SOLES

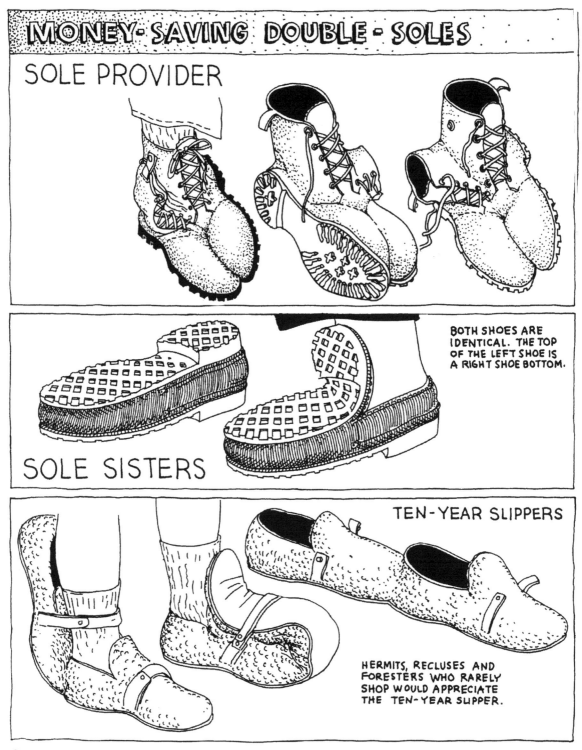

SOLE PROVIDER

SOLE SISTERS

BOTH SHOES ARE IDENTICAL. THE TOP OF THE LEFT SHOE IS A RIGHT SHOE BOTTOM.

TEN-YEAR SLIPPERS

HERMITS, RECLUSES AND FORESTERS WHO RARELY SHOP WOULD APPRECIATE THE TEN-YEAR SLIPPER.

SUMMER/WINTER SHOES

FAMILIES ON TIGHT BUDGETS MAY NEED THESE YEAR-ROUND, WEATHER-RESPONSIVE SHOES. THEY ARE NOT DESIGNED FOR STREAM FORDING OR RAINY DAY WEAR.

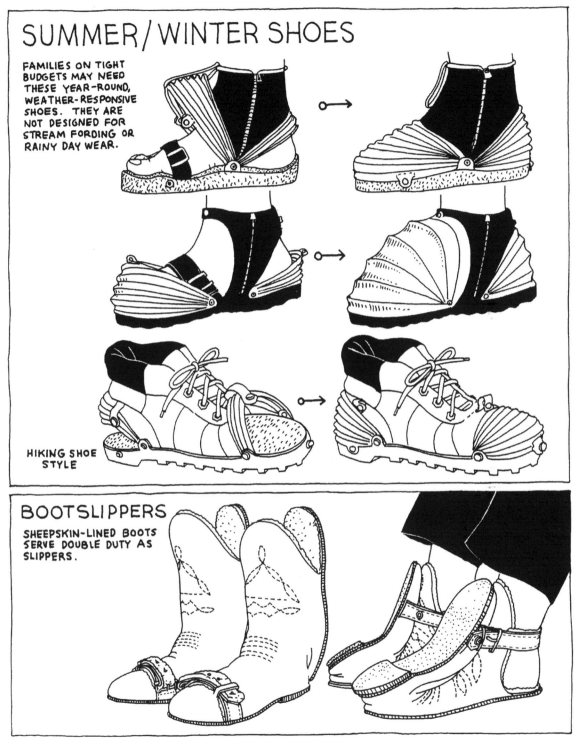

HIKING SHOE STYLE

BOOTSLIPPERS

SHEEPSKIN-LINED BOOTS SERVE DOUBLE DUTY AS SLIPPERS.

THE SELF-MAINTAINING SHOE

BRUSH-UPS

PASTE WAX

SHOE-INS

1.

2.

3.

4.

SHOE TREATS

SPARE HEEL EVENING SHOE

SCREW-ON DECORATIVE FLOWER

HIGH-LOW HEELS

ONE PAIR OF THESE SHOES SUFFICES TO MEET BOTH CASUAL AND SEMI-FORMAL REQUIREMENTS.

FOR CASUAL USE, SIMPLY UNLOCK HEEL.

HEEL-OPTION WALKERS

THE UNIVERSAL SHOE

THE SECRET TO THE UNIVERSAL SHOE IS IN THE PIVOTING DIVIDER WALL. THIS IS THE ONLY SHOE WHICH NEED NOT BE SOLD IN PAIRS. IF A SHOE SHOULD WEAR OUT, GO TO THE SHOE STORE AND BUY A SINGLE SHOE.

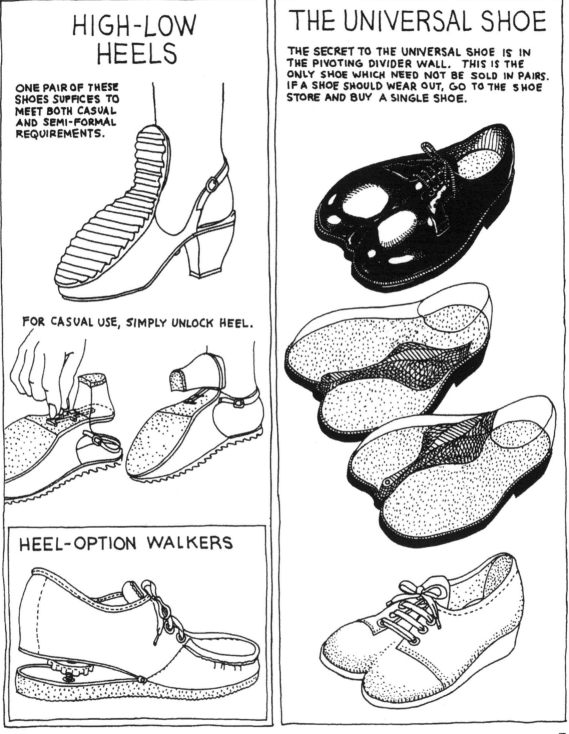

PECULIAR MEN'S SHOES
SHOES WHICH WILL UNFAILINGLY ELICIT COMMENT

EXOTIC WOMEN'S SHOES

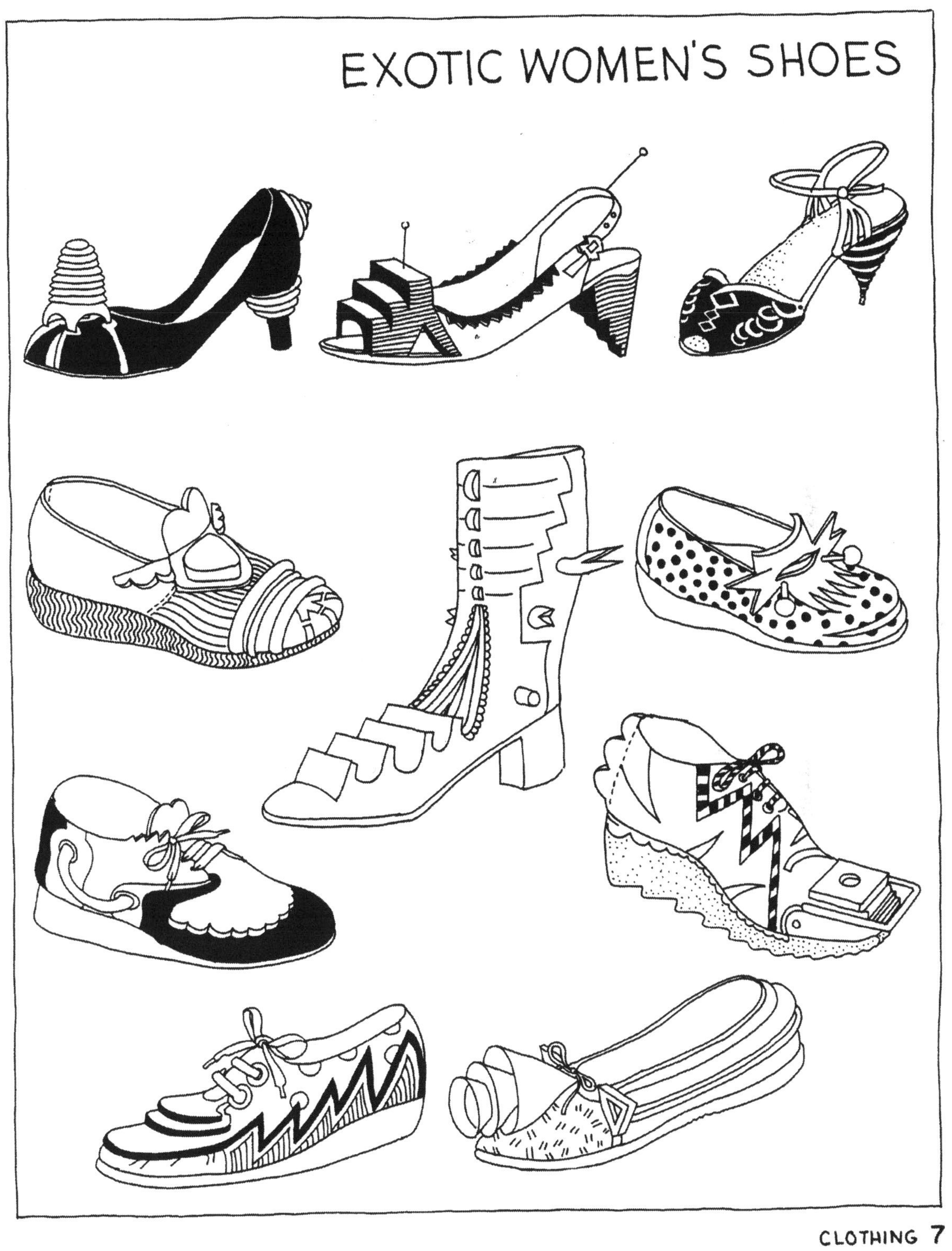

EXTRA-STABILITY SHOES
SHOES ADAPTED TO THE NEEDS OF THE ELDERLY

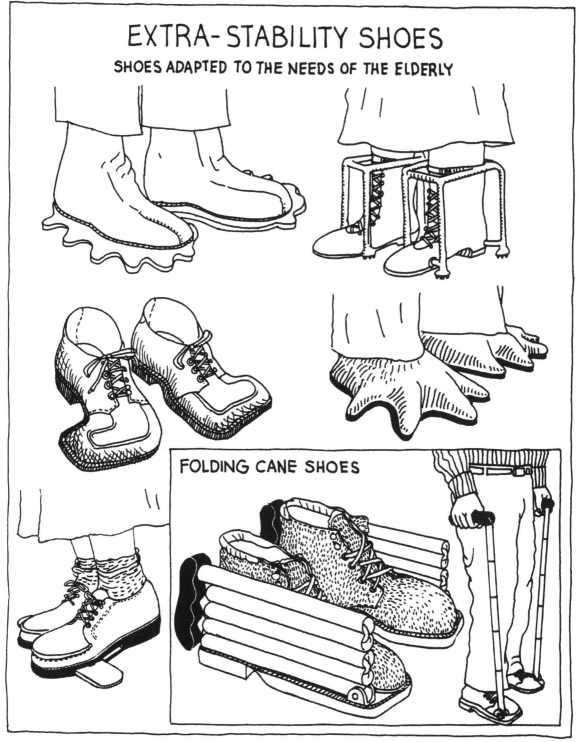

FOLDING CANE SHOES

SHOES FOR
FORMAL OCCASIONS

THESE SHOES ARE
USUALLY WORN WITH
TUXEDOS AND FORMAL
PARTY GOWNS.

WING-TIPS

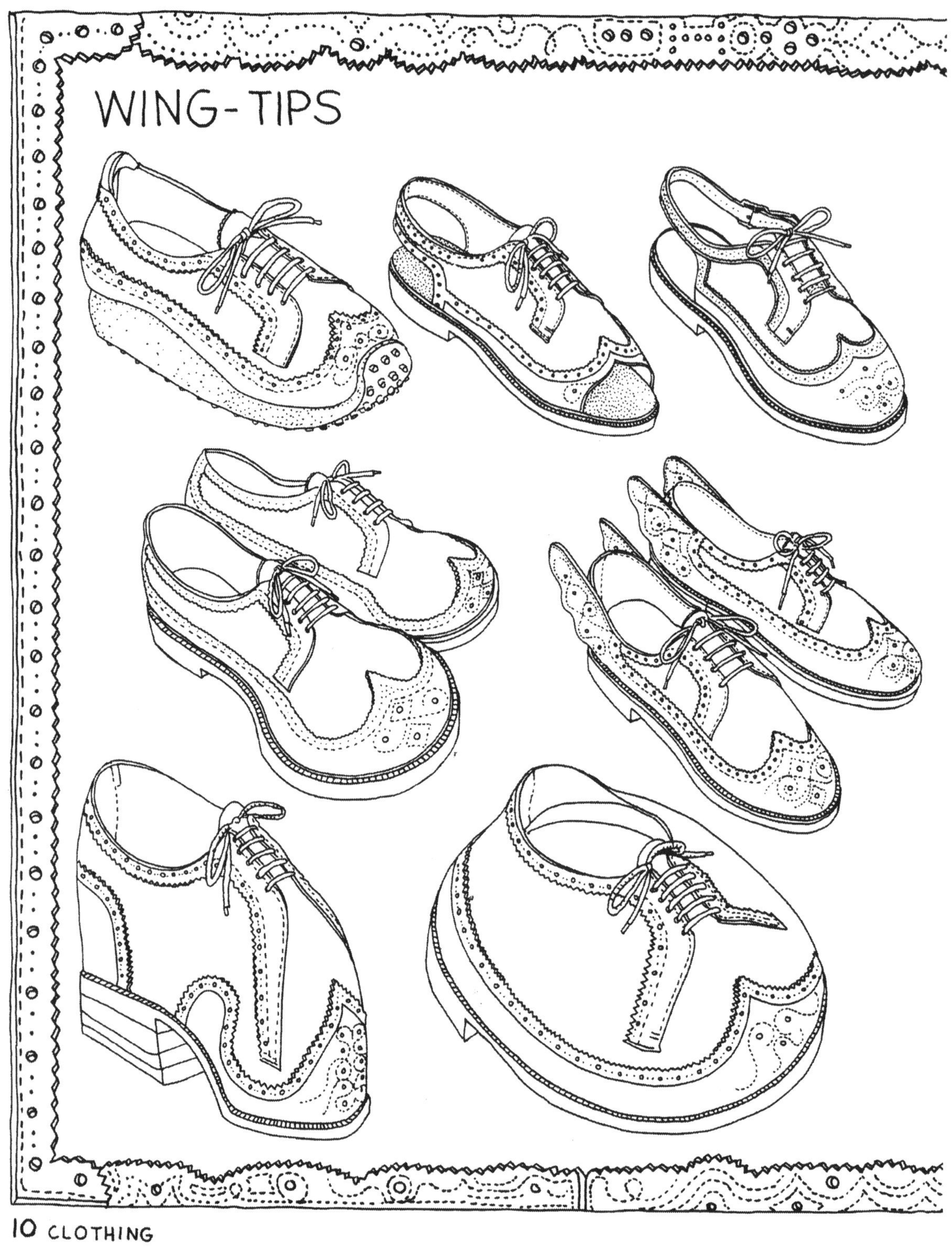

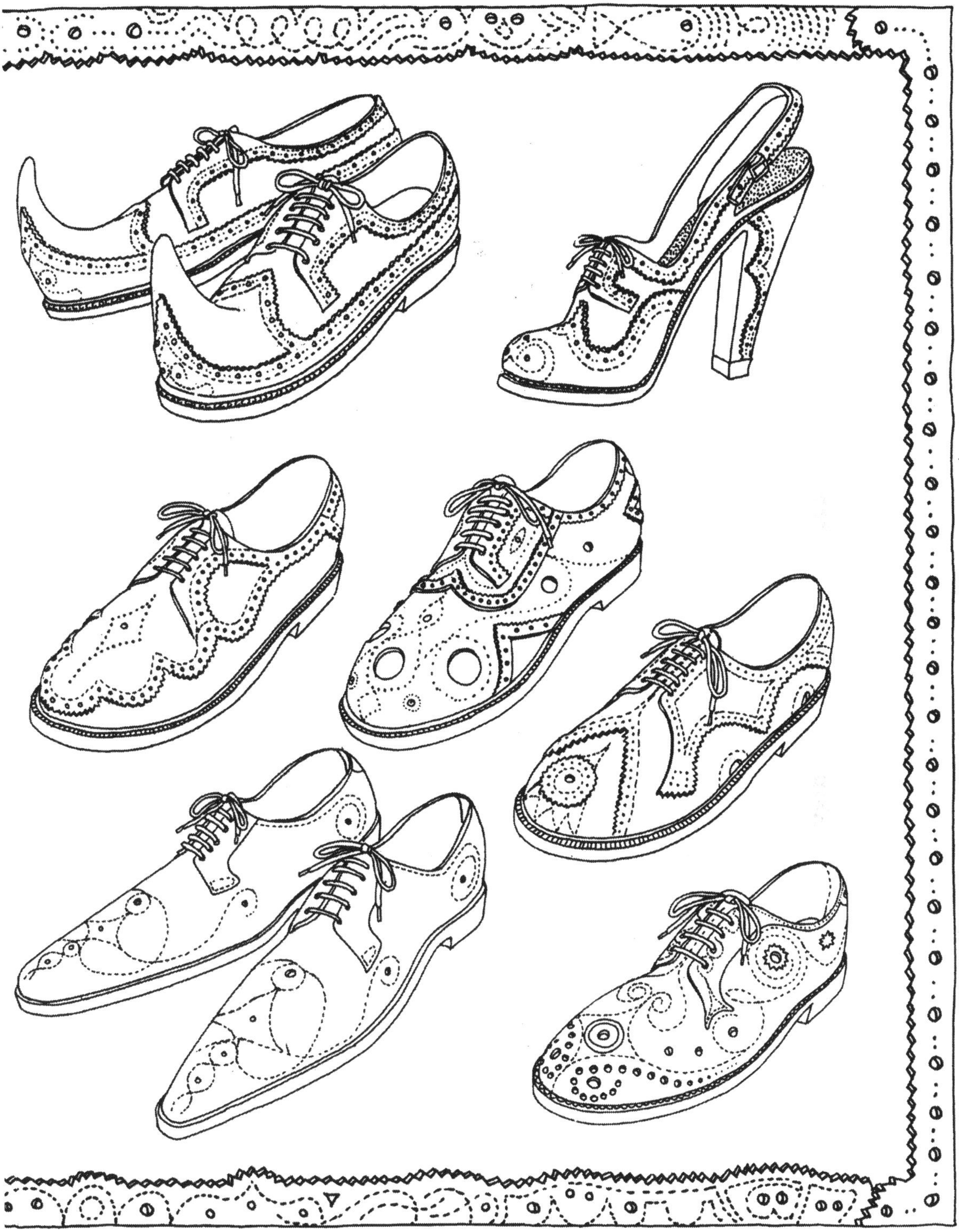

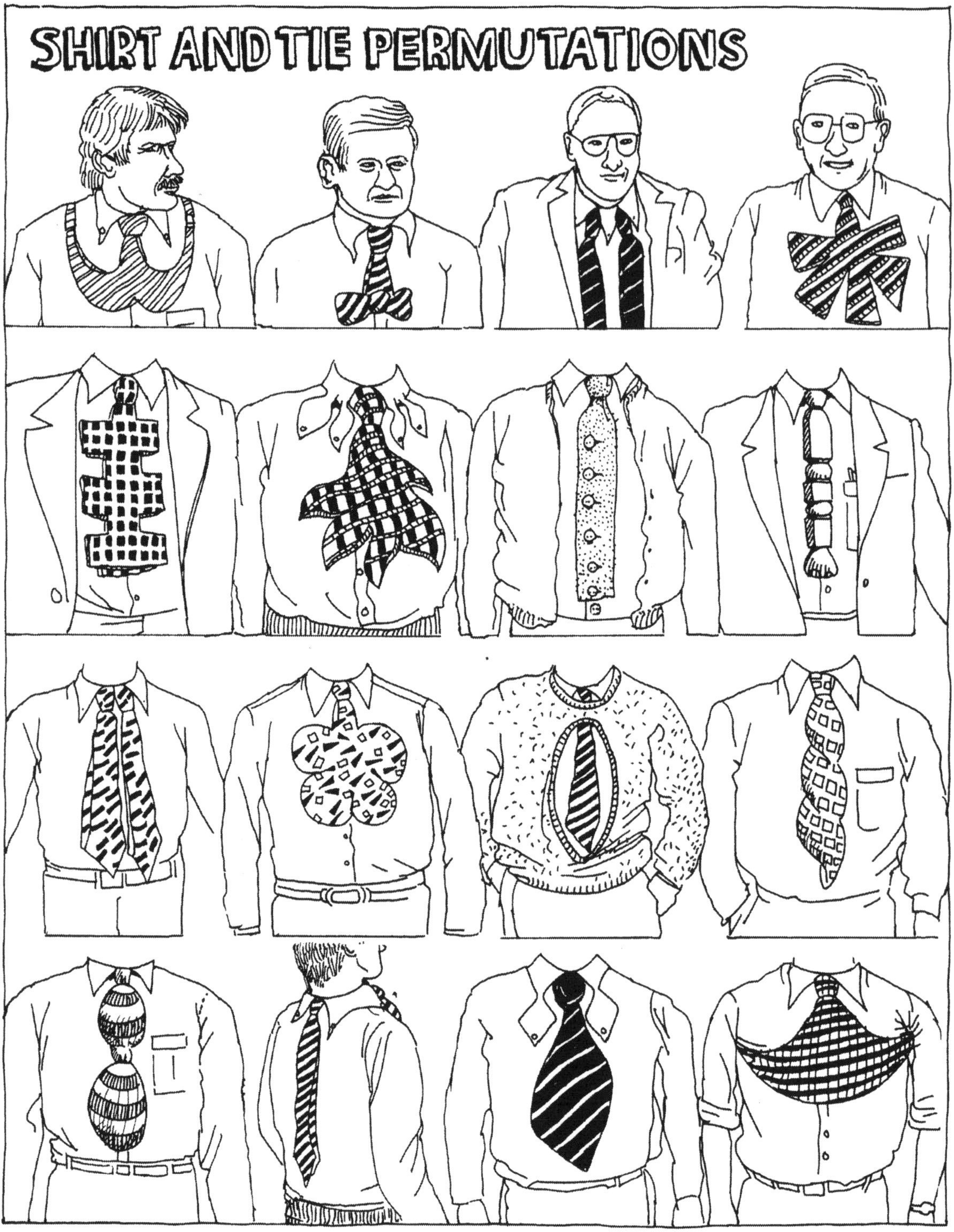
SHIRT AND TIE PERMUTATIONS

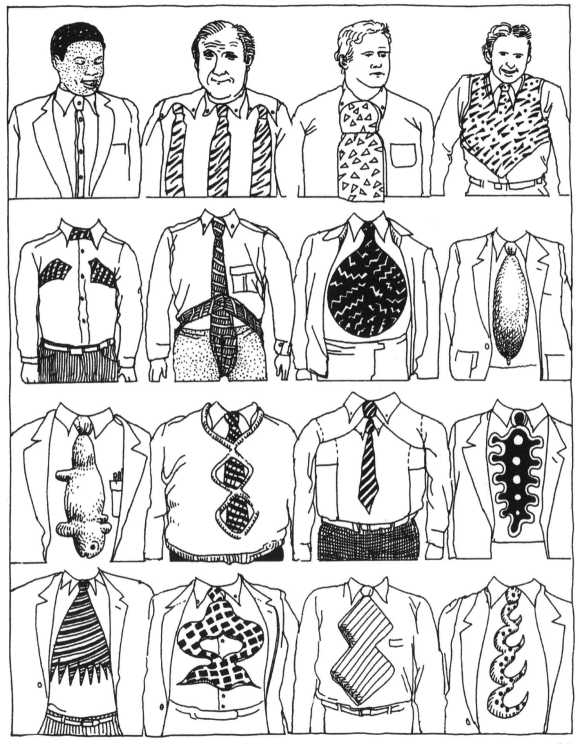

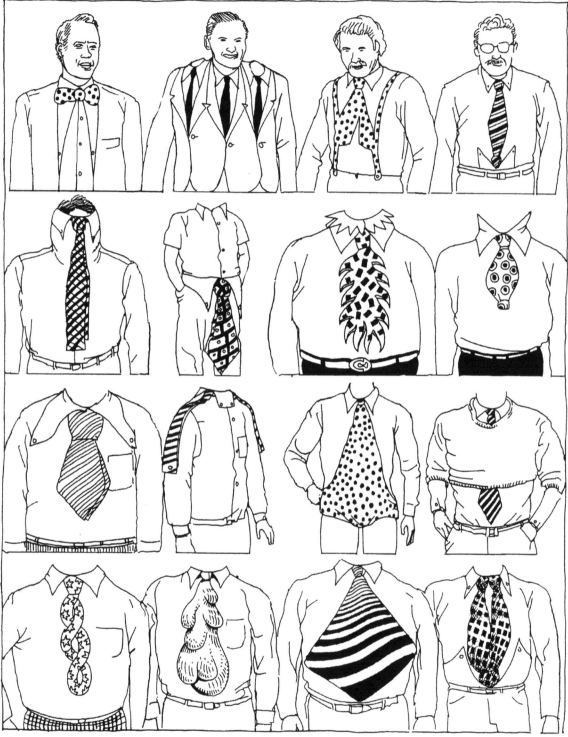

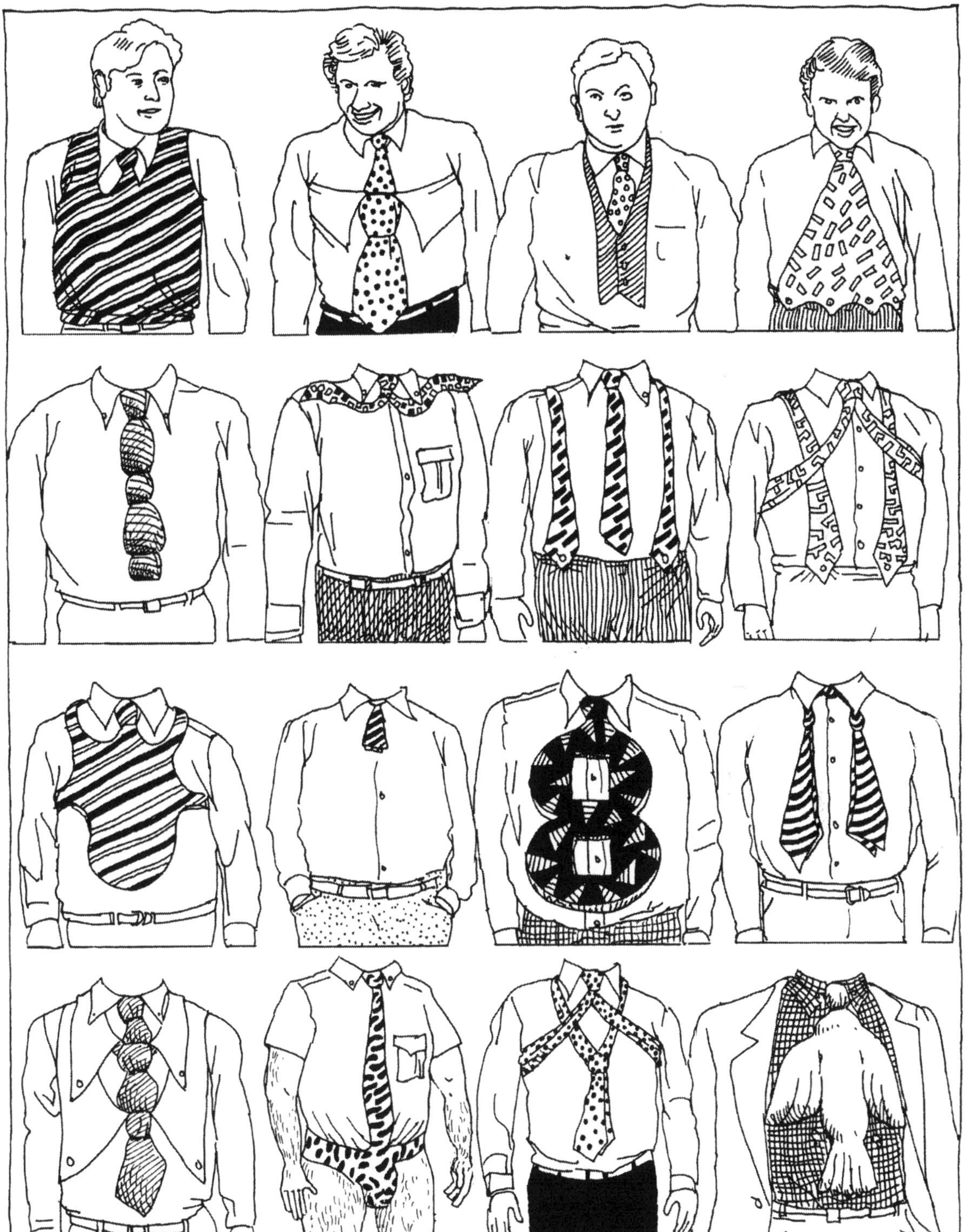

BOLD BUSINESS APPAREL

MEN

PSEUDO-
SLEEVE
POCKETS

WOMEN

BARE
MIDRIFF

ATTACHÉ PURSE

THE *ATTACHÉ PURSE* FRANKLY
ACKNOWLEDGES THE MULTIPLE
LIFE ROLES OF THE MODERN
CAREER WOMAN.

OFFICE JUMPSUIT

MEN

DESIGNED AS A BUSINESS-STYLE COVERALL FOR SHORT NOTICE DINNER DATES, EMERGENCY OFFICE MEETINGS, OR APPOINTMENTS.

PUT ON OVER GARDEN CLOTHES, SWIM SUIT, ATHLETIC APPAREL.

JACKET IS STITCHED TO VEST.

WOMEN

MACHINE-WASHABLE FALSE SHIRT FRONT WITH CONCEALED ZIPPER.

CUFF

HIDDEN ZIPPER

THE BUSINESS SWEAT SUIT

BUSINESS SUIT ENSEMBLES WHICH LOOK
EQUALLY GOOD AT THE OFFICE OR AT
THE FITNESS SPA.

SWEAT SPORTCOAT
AND MATCHING PANTS

DRESS SHIRT
WITH HOOD

SWEAT VEST

TWEED
SWEATS

BRIEFCASE WEAR
HANDS-FREE MINI-OFFICES

BRIEFVEST

BRIEFVEST

THE BRIEFVEST, SHOWN IN TWO STYLES, OFFERS A FOLD-DOWN, BULLET-PROOF WRITING SURFACE.

HARNESS OFFICE

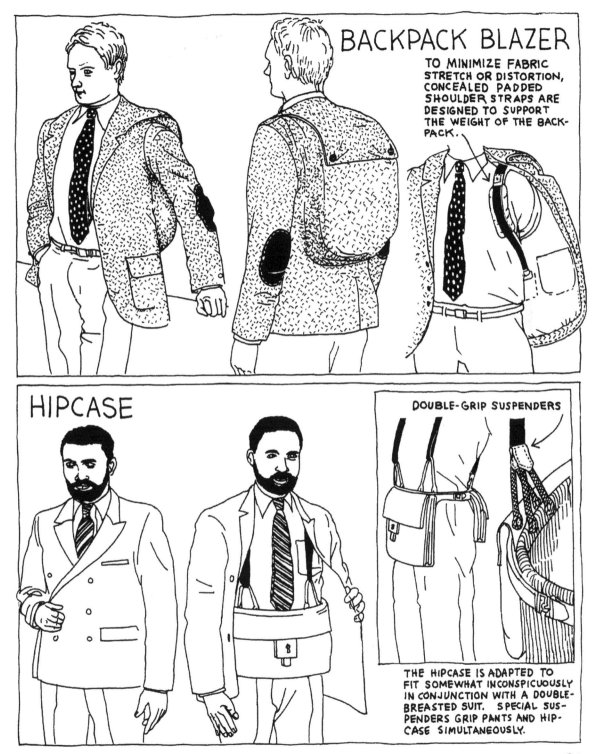

BACKPACK BLAZER

TO MINIMIZE FABRIC STRETCH OR DISTORTION, CONCEALED PADDED SHOULDER STRAPS ARE DESIGNED TO SUPPORT THE WEIGHT OF THE BACK-PACK.

HIPCASE

DOUBLE-GRIP SUSPENDERS

THE HIPCASE IS ADAPTED TO FIT SOMEWHAT INCONSPICUOUSLY IN CONJUNCTION WITH A DOUBLE-BREASTED SUIT. SPECIAL SUS-PENDERS GRIP PANTS AND HIP-CASE SIMULTANEOUSLY.

CLOTHING 21

MULTIPLE-CHOICE APPAREL

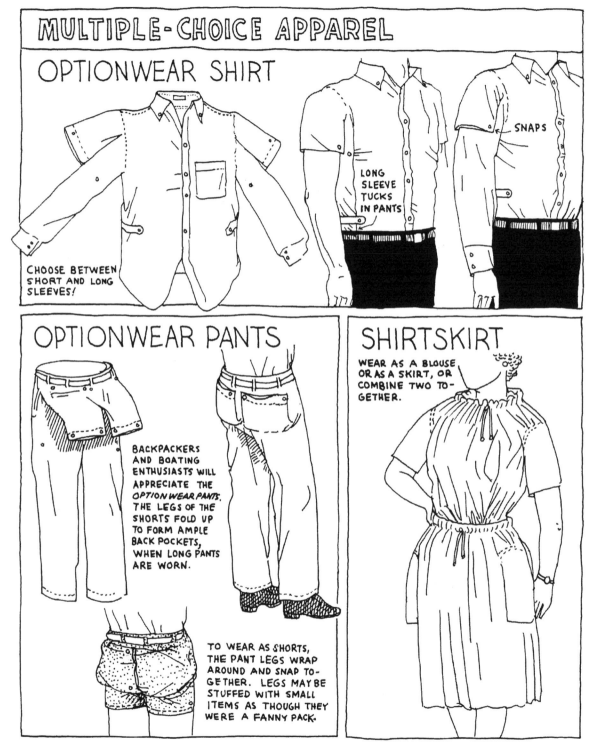

OPTIONWEAR SHIRT

CHOOSE BETWEEN SHORT AND LONG SLEEVES!

LONG SLEEVE TUCKS IN PANTS

SNAPS

OPTIONWEAR PANTS

BACKPACKERS AND BOATING ENTHUSIASTS WILL APPRECIATE THE *OPTIONWEAR PANTS.* THE LEGS OF THE SHORTS FOLD UP TO FORM AMPLE BACK POCKETS, WHEN LONG PANTS ARE WORN.

TO WEAR AS SHORTS, THE PANT LEGS WRAP AROUND AND SNAP TOGETHER. LEGS MAY BE STUFFED WITH SMALL ITEMS AS THOUGH THEY WERE A FANNY PACK.

SHIRTSKIRT

WEAR AS A BLOUSE OR AS A SKIRT, OR COMBINE TWO TOGETHER.

PERSONAL EQUIPMENT

UMBRELLAS

TIEBRELLA

TIEBRELLA, ENCASED IN MATCHING SHEATH, SIMPLY UNSCREWS.

TO RETAIN THE APPEARANCE OF WEARING A TIE, THE SHEATH MAY BE RE-ATTACHED.

UMBRELLA HAT

THE UMBRELLA HAT IS THE ULTIMATE RAINY WEATHER PROTECTION FOR SHOPPERS. BOTH HANDS ARE FREE TO CARRY PACKAGES.

UMBRELLA WITH HOLSTER

THE TRIGGER MECHANISM IN THE ANTIQUE PISTOL HANDLE RELEASES THE SPRING-LOADED UMBRELLA. THE BELT POUCH HOLDS RUBBER OVERSHOES OR FOLDED RAINCOAT.

ARMBRELLA

WORN WITH THE MATCHING DRESS GLOVE, THE ARM-BRELLA IS UNOBTRUSIVE UNDER A COAT SLEEVE.

FOAM-LINED ALUMINUM SHAFT IS VENTILATED.

SPECIALLY-DESIGNED UNDERGARMENT, WITH ONE SHORTER SLEEVE, IS PROVIDED AS PART OF THE OUTFIT.

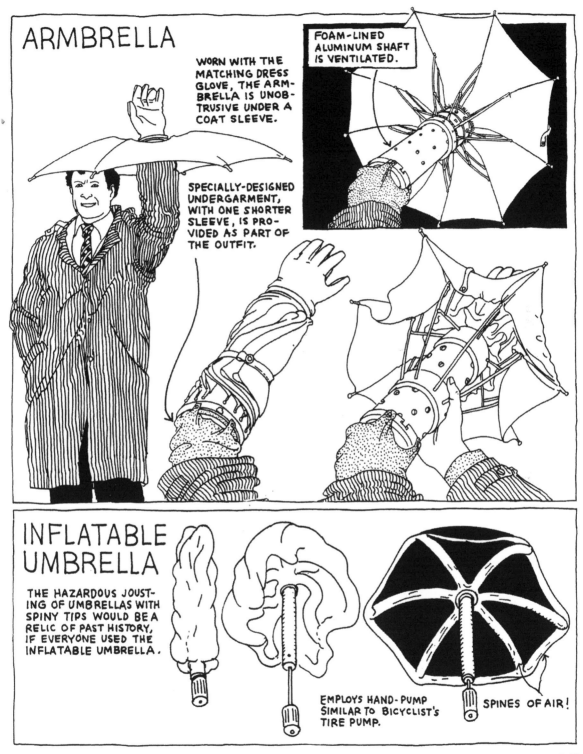

INFLATABLE UMBRELLA

THE HAZARDOUS JOUSTING OF UMBRELLAS WITH SPINY TIPS WOULD BE A RELIC OF PAST HISTORY, IF EVERYONE USED THE INFLATABLE UMBRELLA.

EMPLOYS HAND-PUMP SIMILAR TO BICYCLIST'S TIRE PUMP.

SPINES OF AIR!

RECREATION AND THERAPY

MUSICAL VEST

THE VEST WILL PLAY 27 MAJOR, MINOR OR 7TH CORDS, AND FEATURES FIVE DRUM PATTERNS. FOUR "C" BATTERIES UNDER EACH ARMPIT.

SPEAKER

CASSETTE-PLAYER HELMET

DESIGNED TO MATCH SAFETY STANDARDS FOR BICYCLISTS' HELMETS, BUT MAY BE WORN ANYWHERE.

ACU-HOOD

A CORRECTLY FITTED ACU-HOOD WILL SIMULTANEOUSLY STIMULATE ALL OF THE "ACUPRESSURE" POINTS, LOCATED ALONG THE ENERGY PATHWAYS, OR "MERIDIANS" OF CLASSICAL ACUPUNCTURE THEORY.

INSTANT PHOTO HELMET

ACUPRESSURE POINTS OF THE HEAD

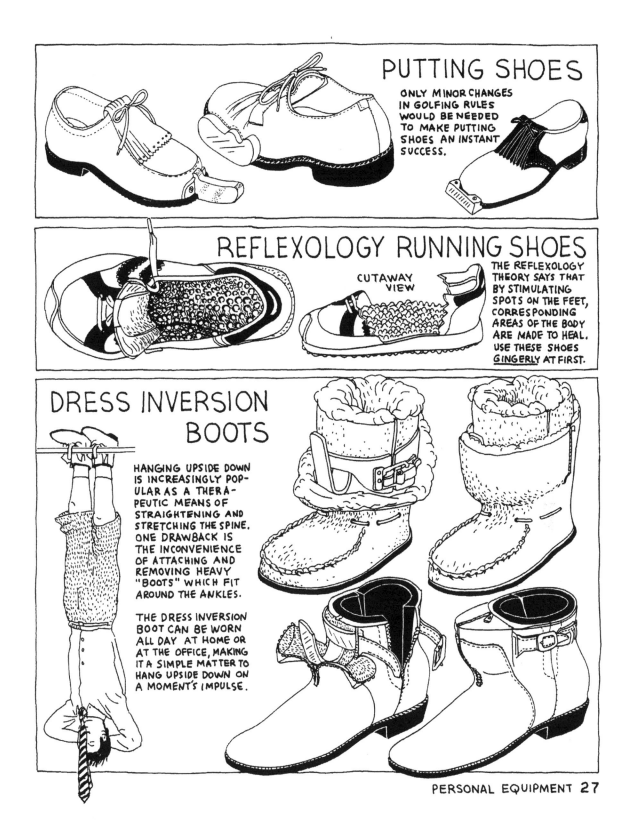

PUTTING SHOES

ONLY MINOR CHANGES IN GOLFING RULES WOULD BE NEEDED TO MAKE PUTTING SHOES AN INSTANT SUCCESS.

REFLEXOLOGY RUNNING SHOES

CUTAWAY VIEW

THE REFLEXOLOGY THEORY SAYS THAT BY STIMULATING SPOTS ON THE FEET, CORRESPONDING AREAS OF THE BODY ARE MADE TO HEAL. USE THESE SHOES GINGERLY AT FIRST.

DRESS INVERSION BOOTS

HANGING UPSIDE DOWN IS INCREASINGLY POP-ULAR AS A THERA-PEUTIC MEANS OF STRAIGHTENING AND STRETCHING THE SPINE. ONE DRAWBACK IS THE INCONVENIENCE OF ATTACHING AND REMOVING HEAVY "BOOTS" WHICH FIT AROUND THE ANKLES.

THE DRESS INVERSION BOOT CAN BE WORN ALL DAY AT HOME OR AT THE OFFICE, MAKING IT A SIMPLE MATTER TO HANG UPSIDE DOWN ON A MOMENT'S IMPULSE.

LIGHTSHOES

SLIPPERSHINES

LIGHTSHOES ASSURE THAT YOUR HANDS ARE FREE WHILE NEGOTIATING HALLWAYS OR BACKWOODS TRAILS AT NIGHT. MOST SOPHISTICATED IS THE *SLIPPERSHINE* SERIES. *SLIPPERSHINES* ARE PARKED AT ALL TIMES IN A RE-CHARGING STATION. ILLUMINATED HEEL LOCATORS, L AND H, ARE PRESSURE-SENSITIVE LIGHTSWITCHES.

PLUG-INS

PLUG-INS OFFER FEWER FEATURES THAN *SLIPPERSHINES*, BUT REQUIRE LESS APPARATUS. THE SHOES, WITH NIGHTLIGHT, SIMPLY PLUG INTO ANY SOCKET TO RECHARGE THE NI-CAD BATTERIES.

SELF-GENERATING LIGHT SHOES COME IN TWO STYLES: (A) COMPRESSION OF HEEL WORKS GENERATOR, (B) HEAVY "FLY HEEL" SPINS TO GENERATE LIGHT.

BATTERY-OPERATED LIGHTSHOES.

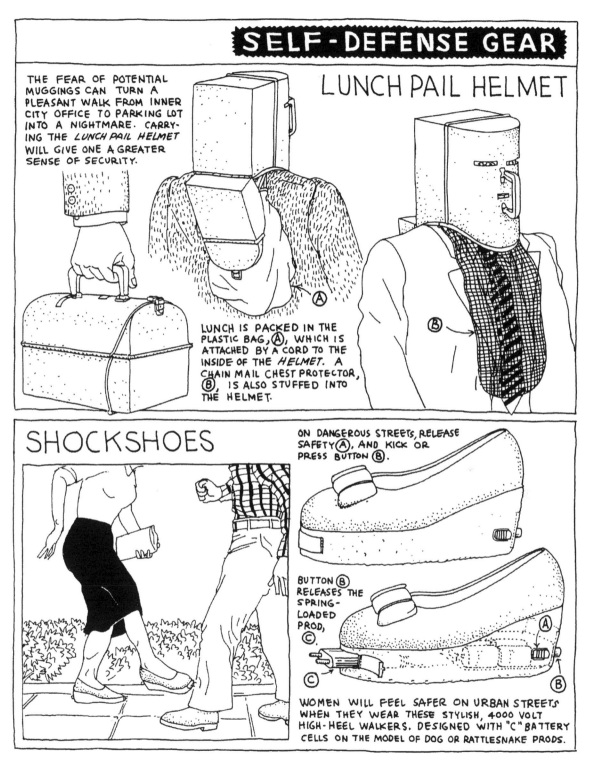

SELF-DEFENSE GEAR

LUNCH PAIL HELMET

THE FEAR OF POTENTIAL MUGGINGS CAN TURN A PLEASANT WALK FROM INNER CITY OFFICE TO PARKING LOT INTO A NIGHTMARE. CARRYING THE *LUNCH PAIL HELMET* WILL GIVE ONE A GREATER SENSE OF SECURITY.

LUNCH IS PACKED IN THE PLASTIC BAG, Ⓐ, WHICH IS ATTACHED BY A CORD TO THE INSIDE OF THE *HELMET.* A CHAIN MAIL CHEST PROTECTOR, Ⓑ, IS ALSO STUFFED INTO THE HELMET.

SHOCKSHOES

ON DANGEROUS STREETS, RELEASE SAFETY Ⓐ, AND KICK OR PRESS BUTTON Ⓑ.

BUTTON Ⓑ RELEASES THE SPRING-LOADED PROD, Ⓒ.

WOMEN WILL FEEL SAFER ON URBAN STREETS WHEN THEY WEAR THESE STYLISH, 4000 VOLT HIGH-HEEL WALKERS. DESIGNED WITH "C" BATTERY CELLS ON THE MODEL OF DOG OR RATTLESNAKE PRODS.

WORKSHOP SHOES

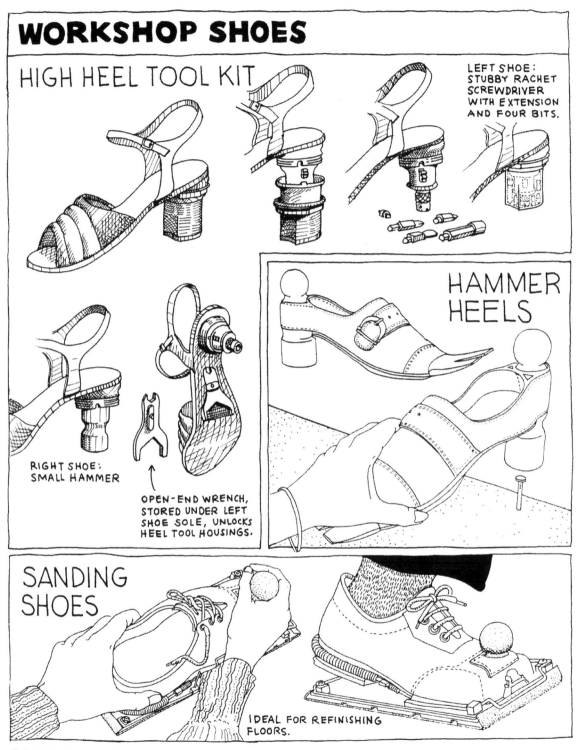

HIGH HEEL TOOL KIT

LEFT SHOE: STUBBY RACHET SCREWDRIVER WITH EXTENSION AND FOUR BITS.

RIGHT SHOE: SMALL HAMMER

OPEN-END WRENCH, STORED UNDER LEFT SHOE SOLE, UNLOCKS HEEL TOOL HOUSINGS.

HAMMER HEELS

SANDING SHOES

IDEAL FOR REFINISHING FLOORS.

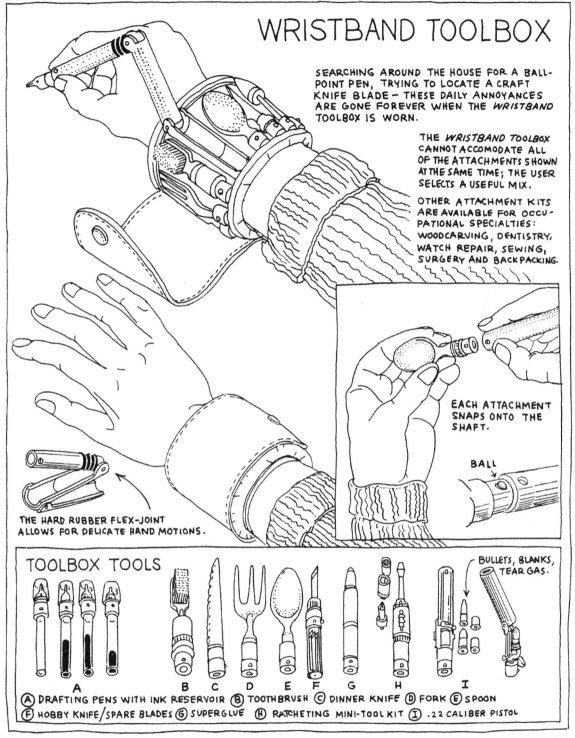

WRISTBAND TOOLBOX

SEARCHING AROUND THE HOUSE FOR A BALL-POINT PEN, TRYING TO LOCATE A CRAFT KNIFE BLADE – THESE DAILY ANNOYANCES ARE GONE FOREVER WHEN THE *WRISTBAND TOOLBOX* IS WORN.

THE *WRISTBAND TOOLBOX* CANNOT ACCOMODATE ALL OF THE ATTACHMENTS SHOWN AT THE SAME TIME; THE USER SELECTS A USEFUL MIX.

OTHER ATTACHMENT KITS ARE AVAILABLE FOR OCCUPATIONAL SPECIALTIES: WOODCARVING, DENTISTRY, WATCH REPAIR, SEWING, SURGERY AND BACKPACKING.

EACH ATTACHMENT SNAPS ONTO THE SHAFT.

BALL

THE HARD RUBBER FLEX-JOINT ALLOWS FOR DELICATE HAND MOTIONS.

TOOLBOX TOOLS

BULLETS, BLANKS, TEAR GAS.

Ⓐ DRAFTING PENS WITH INK RESERVOIR Ⓑ TOOTHBRUSH Ⓒ DINNER KNIFE Ⓓ FORK Ⓔ SPOON
Ⓕ HOBBY KNIFE/SPARE BLADES Ⓖ SUPERGLUE Ⓗ RATCHETING MINI-TOOL KIT Ⓘ .22 CALIBER PISTOL

HIGH-TECH

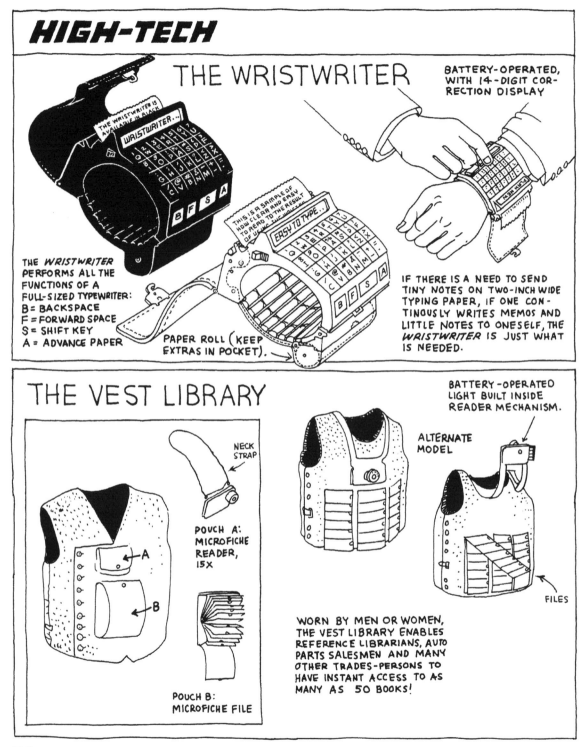

THE WRISTWRITER

BATTERY-OPERATED, WITH 14-DIGIT CORRECTION DISPLAY

THE WRISTWRITER IS AVAILABLE IN BLACK.

WRISTWRITER

THIS IS A SAMPLE OF HOW CLEAR AND EASY TO READ TO THE RESULT OF USING THE WRISTWRITER

EASY TO TYPE

THE *WRISTWRITER* PERFORMS ALL THE FUNCTIONS OF A FULL-SIZED TYPEWRITER:
B = BACKSPACE
F = FORWARD SPACE
S = SHIFT KEY
A = ADVANCE PAPER

PAPER ROLL (KEEP EXTRAS IN POCKET).

IF THERE IS A NEED TO SEND TINY NOTES ON TWO-INCH WIDE TYPING PAPER, IF ONE CONTINOUSLY WRITES MEMOS AND LITTLE NOTES TO ONESELF, THE *WRISTWRITER* IS JUST WHAT IS NEEDED.

THE VEST LIBRARY

BATTERY-OPERATED LIGHT BUILT INSIDE READER MECHANISM.

ALTERNATE MODEL

NECK STRAP

POUCH A: MICROFICHE READER, 15X

A

B

FILES

POUCH B: MICROFICHE FILE

WORN BY MEN OR WOMEN, THE VEST LIBRARY ENABLES REFERENCE LIBRARIANS, AUTO PARTS SALESMEN AND MANY OTHER TRADES-PERSONS TO HAVE INSTANT ACCESS TO AS MANY AS 50 BOOKS!

CORDLESS PHONE DIRECTORY

CURRENTLY, THE USE OF CORDLESS PHONES IS LIMITED BY THE INCONVENIENCE OF LUGGING A FIVE-POUND PHONE DIRECTORY AROUND THE BLOCK OR AROUND THE POOLSIDE. THIS CORDLESS PHONE, WITH A BUILT-IN MICROFICHE PHONE DIRECTORY, SOLVES THE PROBLEM!

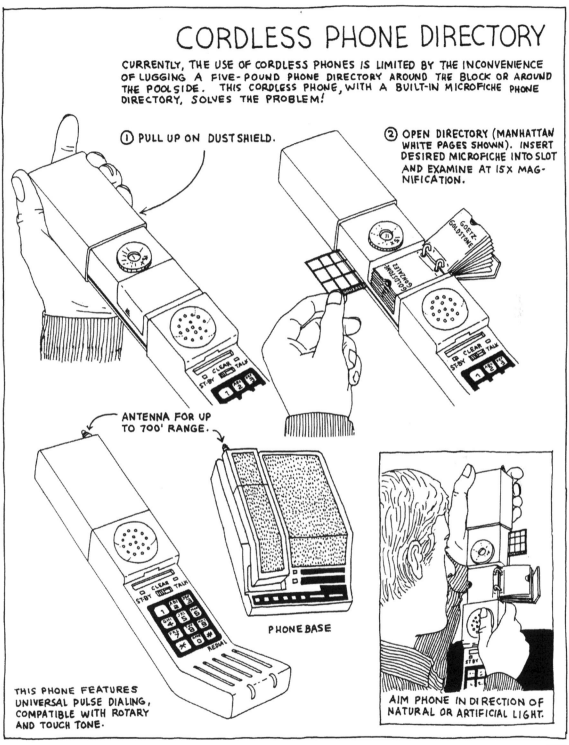

① PULL UP ON DUST SHIELD.

② OPEN DIRECTORY (MANHATTAN WHITE PAGES SHOWN). INSERT DESIRED MICROFICHE INTO SLOT AND EXAMINE AT 15X MAGNIFICATION.

ANTENNA FOR UP TO 700' RANGE.

PHONE BASE

THIS PHONE FEATURES UNIVERSAL PULSE DIALING, COMPATIBLE WITH ROTARY AND TOUCH TONE.

AIM PHONE IN DIRECTION OF NATURAL OR ARTIFICIAL LIGHT.

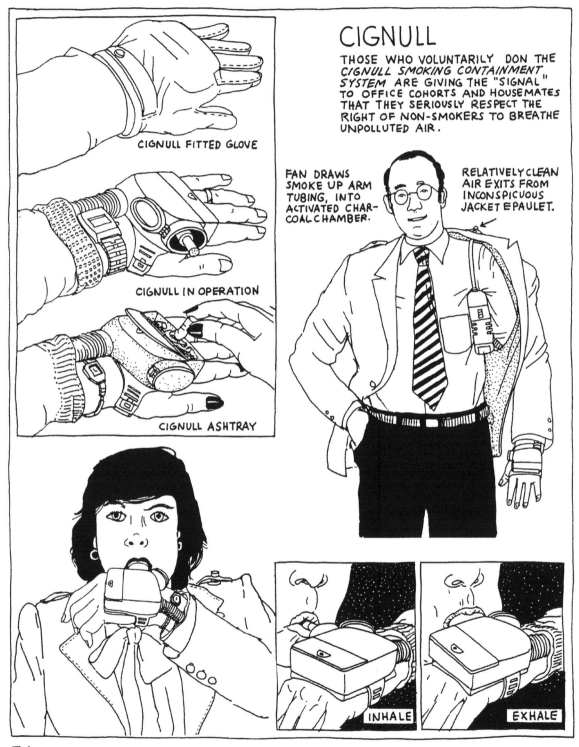

CIGNULL

THOSE WHO VOLUNTARILY DON THE *CIGNULL SMOKING CONTAINMENT SYSTEM* ARE GIVING THE "SIGNAL" TO OFFICE COHORTS AND HOUSEMATES THAT THEY SERIOUSLY RESPECT THE RIGHT OF NON-SMOKERS TO BREATHE UNPOLLUTED AIR.

CIGNULL FITTED GLOVE

CIGNULL IN OPERATION

CIGNULL ASHTRAY

FAN DRAWS SMOKE UP ARM TUBING, INTO ACTIVATED CHARCOAL CHAMBER.

RELATIVELY CLEAN AIR EXITS FROM INCONSPICUOUS JACKET EPAULET.

INHALE

EXHALE

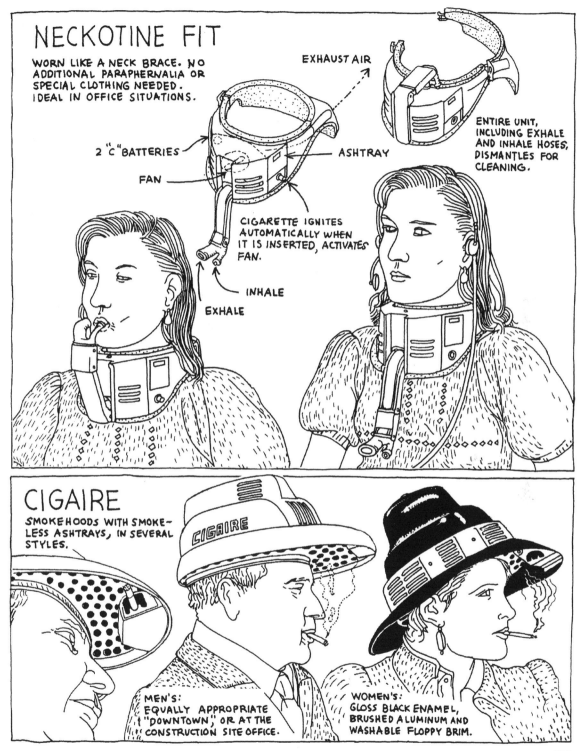

NECKOTINE FIT

WORN LIKE A NECK BRACE. NO ADDITIONAL PARAPHERNALIA OR SPECIAL CLOTHING NEEDED. IDEAL IN OFFICE SITUATIONS.

EXHAUST AIR

ENTIRE UNIT, INCLUDING EXHALE AND INHALE HOSES, DISMANTLES FOR CLEANING.

2 "C" BATTERIES

ASHTRAY

FAN

CIGARETTE IGNITES AUTOMATICALLY WHEN IT IS INSERTED, ACTIVATES FAN.

INHALE

EXHALE

CIGAIRE

SMOKEHOODS WITH SMOKE-LESS ASHTRAYS, IN SEVERAL STYLES.

CIGAIRE

MEN'S: EQUALLY APPROPRIATE "DOWNTOWN" OR AT THE CONSTRUCTION SITE OFFICE.

WOMEN'S: GLOSS BLACK ENAMEL, BRUSHED ALUMINUM AND WASHABLE FLOPPY BRIM.

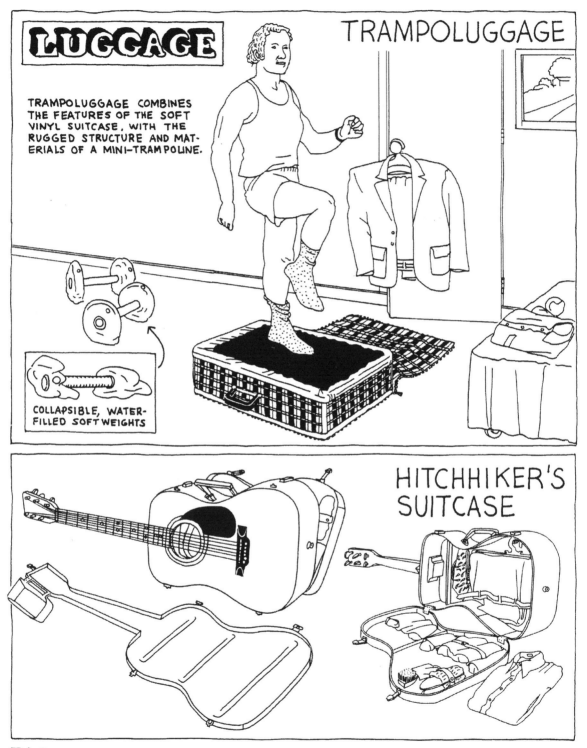

LUGGAGE

TRAMPOLUGGAGE

TRAMPOLUGGAGE COMBINES THE FEATURES OF THE SOFT VINYL SUITCASE, WITH THE RUGGED STRUCTURE AND MATERIALS OF A MINI-TRAMPOLINE.

COLLAPSIBLE, WATER-FILLED SOFT WEIGHTS

HITCHHIKER'S SUITCASE

"SITCASES" FOR BUS DEPOTS AND AIRPORT WAITING ROOMS

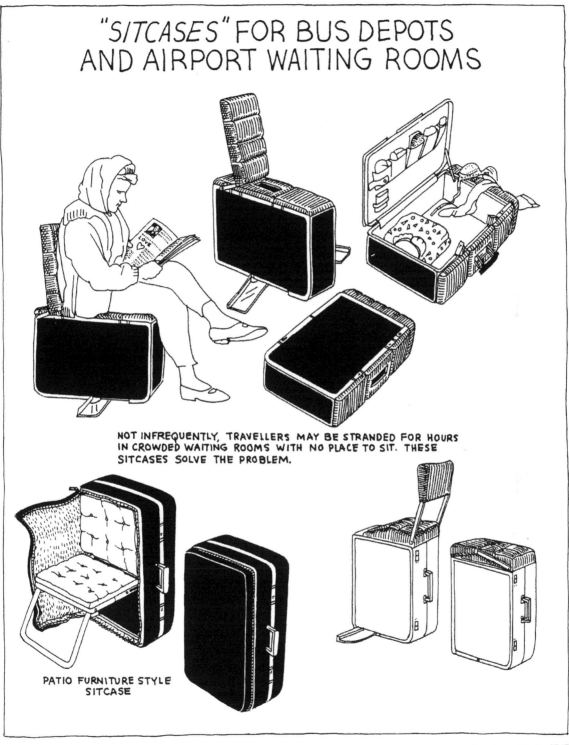

NOT INFREQUENTLY, TRAVELLERS MAY BE STRANDED FOR HOURS IN CROWDED WAITING ROOMS WITH NO PLACE TO SIT. THESE SITCASES SOLVE THE PROBLEM.

PATIO FURNITURE STYLE SITCASE

THE SPARE PAIR OF SUNGLASSES

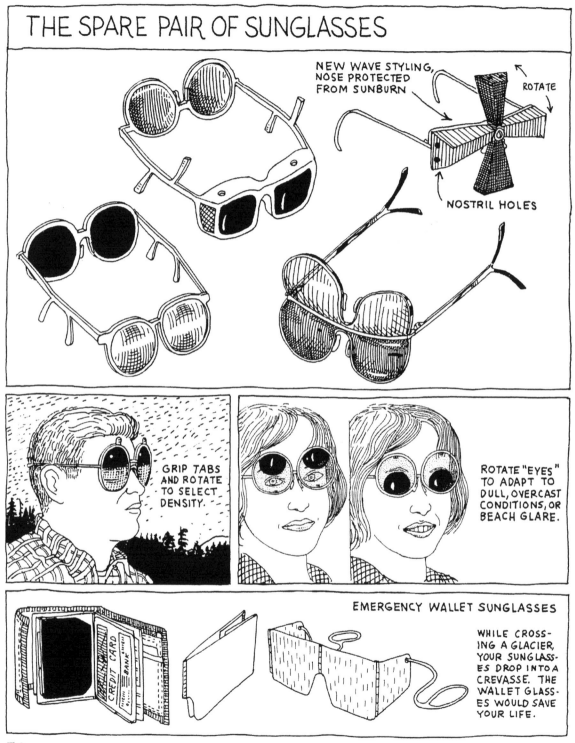

NEW WAVE STYLING, NOSE PROTECTED FROM SUNBURN

ROTATE

NOSTRIL HOLES

GRIP TABS AND ROTATE TO SELECT DENSITY.

ROTATE "EYES" TO ADAPT TO DULL, OVERCAST CONDITIONS, OR BEACH GLARE.

EMERGENCY WALLET SUNGLASSES

WHILE CROSSING A GLACIER, YOUR SUNGLASSES DROP INTO A CREVASSE. THE WALLET GLASSES WOULD SAVE YOUR LIFE.

MULTIPLE-CHOICE SUNGLASSES

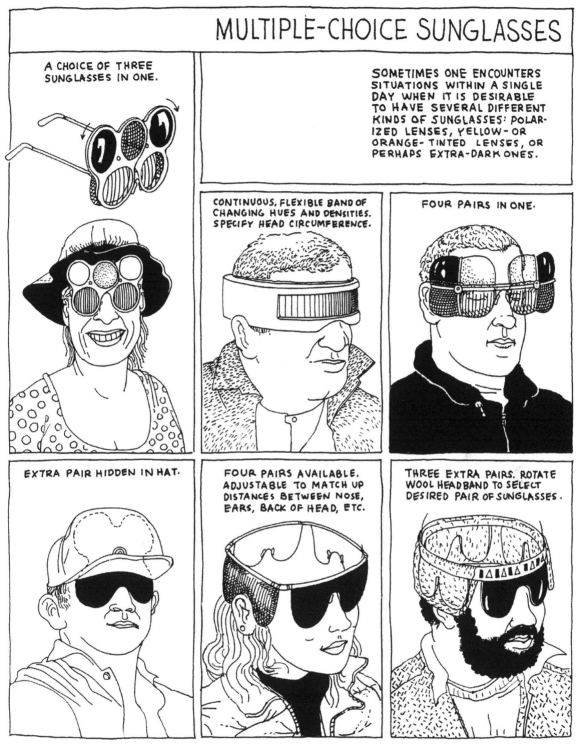

A CHOICE OF THREE SUNGLASSES IN ONE.

SOMETIMES ONE ENCOUNTERS SITUATIONS WITHIN A SINGLE DAY WHEN IT IS DESIRABLE TO HAVE SEVERAL DIFFERENT KINDS OF SUNGLASSES: POLARIZED LENSES, YELLOW- OR ORANGE- TINTED LENSES, OR PERHAPS EXTRA-DARK ONES.

CONTINUOUS, FLEXIBLE BAND OF CHANGING HUES AND DENSITIES. SPECIFY HEAD CIRCUMFERENCE.

FOUR PAIRS IN ONE.

EXTRA PAIR HIDDEN IN HAT.

FOUR PAIRS AVAILABLE. ADJUSTABLE TO MATCH UP DISTANCES BETWEEN NOSE, EARS, BACK OF HEAD, ETC.

THREE EXTRA PAIRS. ROTATE WOOL HEADBAND TO SELECT DESIRED PAIR OF SUNGLASSES.

NEW WAYS TO HOLD GLASSES IN PLACE

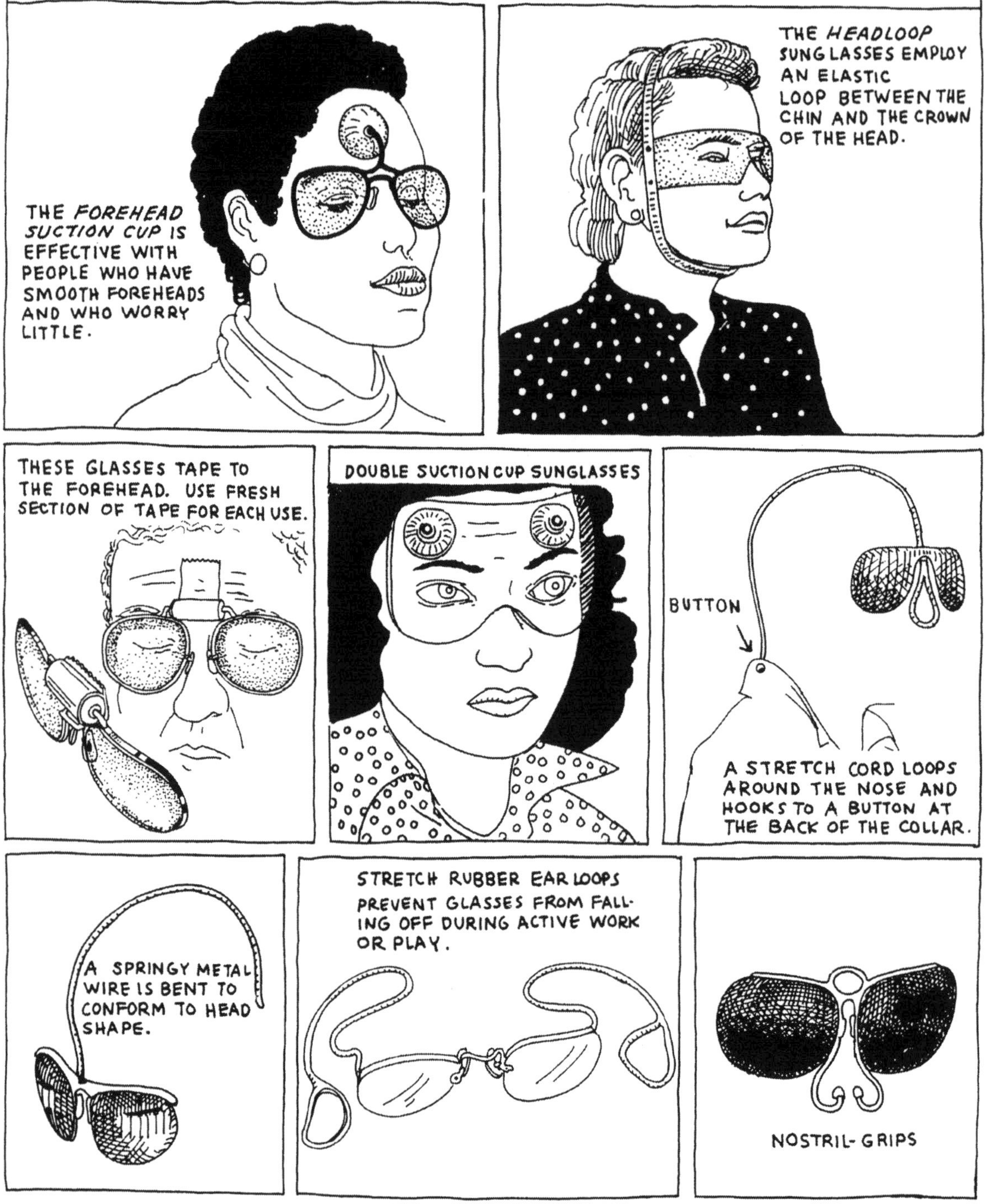
THE FOREHEAD SUCTION CUP IS EFFECTIVE WITH PEOPLE WHO HAVE SMOOTH FOREHEADS AND WHO WORRY LITTLE.
THE HEADLOOP SUNGLASSES EMPLOY AN ELASTIC LOOP BETWEEN THE CHIN AND THE CROWN OF THE HEAD.
THESE GLASSES TAPE TO THE FOREHEAD. USE FRESH SECTION OF TAPE FOR EACH USE.
DOUBLE SUCTION CUP SUNGLASSES
BUTTON
A STRETCH CORD LOOPS AROUND THE NOSE AND HOOKS TO A BUTTON AT THE BACK OF THE COLLAR.
A SPRINGY METAL WIRE IS BENT TO CONFORM TO HEAD SHAPE.
STRETCH RUBBER EAR LOOPS PREVENT GLASSES FROM FALLING OFF DURING ACTIVE WORK OR PLAY.
NOSTRIL-GRIPS

GLASSES NEVER OUT OF REACH

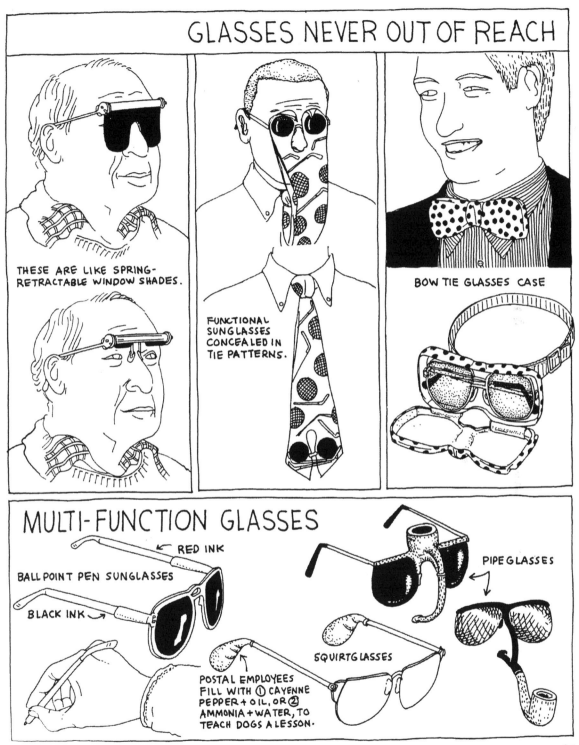

THESE ARE LIKE SPRING-RETRACTABLE WINDOW SHADES.

FUNCTIONAL SUNGLASSES CONCEALED IN TIE PATTERNS.

BOW TIE GLASSES CASE

MULTI-FUNCTION GLASSES

RED INK

BALL POINT PEN SUNGLASSES

BLACK INK →

PIPE GLASSES

SQUIRT GLASSES

POSTAL EMPLOYEES FILL WITH ① CAYENNE PEPPER + OIL, OR ② AMMONIA + WATER, TO TEACH DOGS A LESSON.

FUNGLASSES

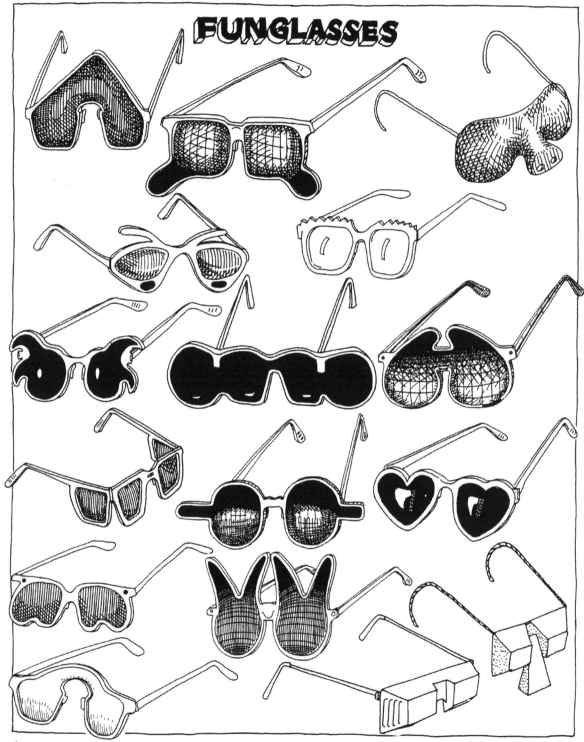

DINING TECHNOLOGY

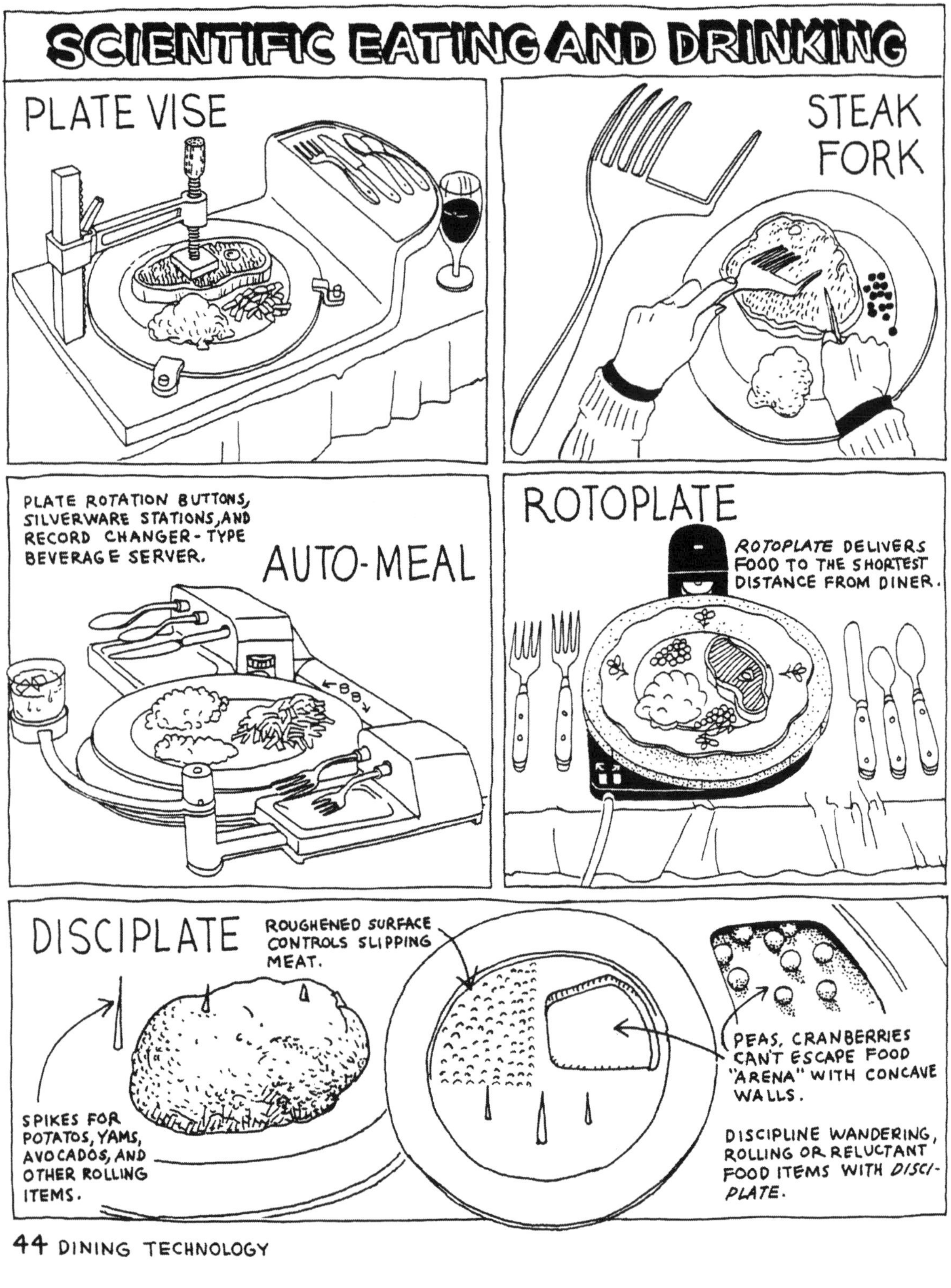
SCIENTIFIC EATING AND DRINKING
PLATE VISE
STEAK FORK
PLATE ROTATION BUTTONS, SILVERWARE STATIONS, AND RECORD CHANGER-TYPE BEVERAGE SERVER.
AUTO-MEAL
ROTOPLATE
ROTOPLATE DELIVERS FOOD TO THE SHORTEST DISTANCE FROM DINER.
DISCIPLATE
ROUGHENED SURFACE CONTROLS SLIPPING MEAT.
SPIKES FOR POTATOS, YAMS, AVOCADOS, AND OTHER ROLLING ITEMS.
PEAS, CRANBERRIES CAN'T ESCAPE FOOD "ARENA" WITH CONCAVE WALLS.
DISCIPLINE WANDERING, ROLLING OR RELUCTANT FOOD ITEMS WITH DISCI-PLATE.

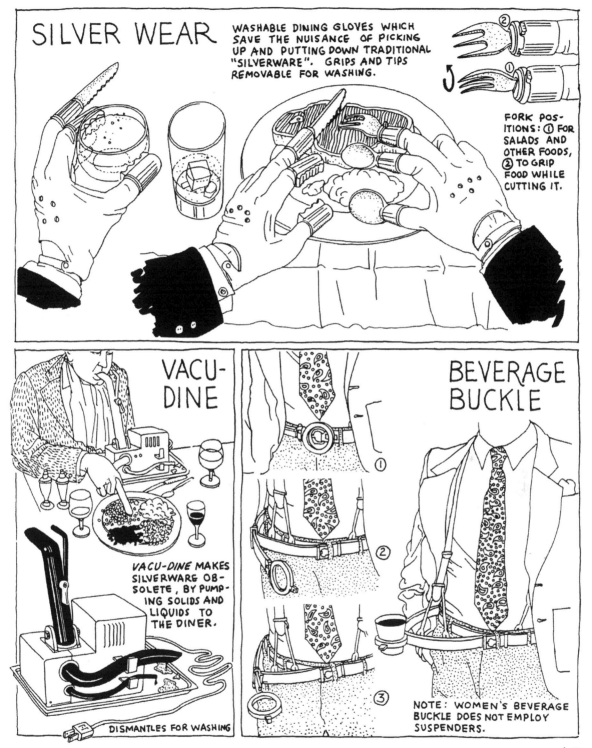

SILVER WEAR

WASHABLE DINING GLOVES WHICH SAVE THE NUISANCE OF PICKING UP AND PUTTING DOWN TRADITIONAL "SILVERWARE". GRIPS AND TIPS REMOVABLE FOR WASHING.

FORK POSITIONS: ① FOR SALADS AND OTHER FOODS, ② TO GRIP FOOD WHILE CUTTING IT.

VACU-DINE

VACU-DINE MAKES SILVERWARE OBSOLETE, BY PUMPING SOLIDS AND LIQUIDS TO THE DINER.

DISMANTLES FOR WASHING

BEVERAGE BUCKLE

NOTE: WOMEN'S BEVERAGE BUCKLE DOES NOT EMPLOY SUSPENDERS.

DINING TECHNOLOGY 45

DINING PARAPHERNALIA
NEW SILVERWARE CONCEPTS

BURGERGRIP

NO-FAULT CHOPSTICKS

NO-FAULT CHOPSTICKS ARE FULLY AUTOMATIC AND REQUIRE NO LESSONS. USING THESE ONE CAN FORGET THE FATIGUING BATTLES WITH UNFAMILIAR CHOPSTICKS (TONG WARS).

CONDIMENT LAUNCH

SPRING-LOADED LAUNCHER CASTS A FAVORITE CONDIMENT OVER A BITE OF FOOD.

FRANKGRIP

ELEGANT HOTDOG HOLDER

FOOD MAGNIFIER

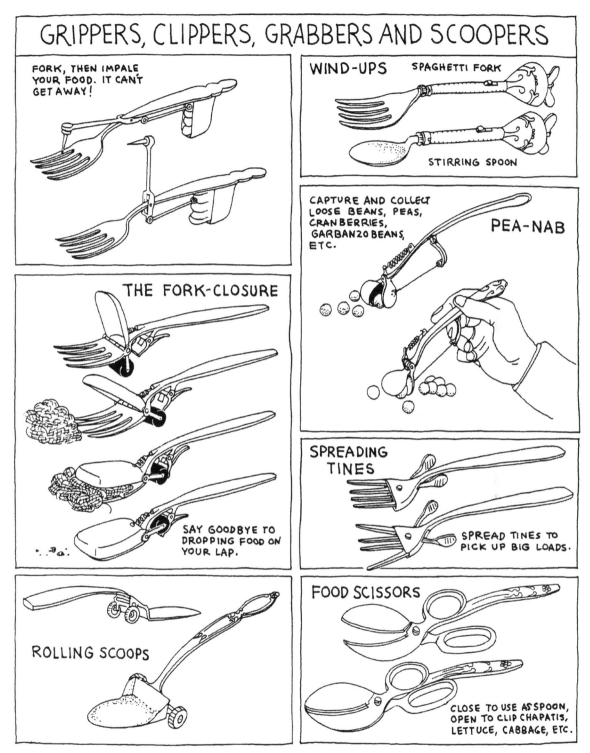

GRIPPERS, CLIPPERS, GRABBERS AND SCOOPERS

FORK, THEN IMPALE YOUR FOOD. IT CAN'T GET AWAY!

WIND-UPS

SPAGHETTI FORK

STIRRING SPOON

CAPTURE AND COLLECT LOOSE BEANS, PEAS, CRANBERRIES, GARBANZO BEANS, ETC.

PEA-NAB

THE FORK-CLOSURE

SAY GOODBYE TO DROPPING FOOD ON YOUR LAP.

SPREADING TINES

SPREAD TINES TO PICK UP BIG LOADS.

ROLLING SCOOPS

FOOD SCISSORS

CLOSE TO USE AS SPOON, OPEN TO CLIP CHAPATIS, LETTUCE, CABBAGE, ETC.

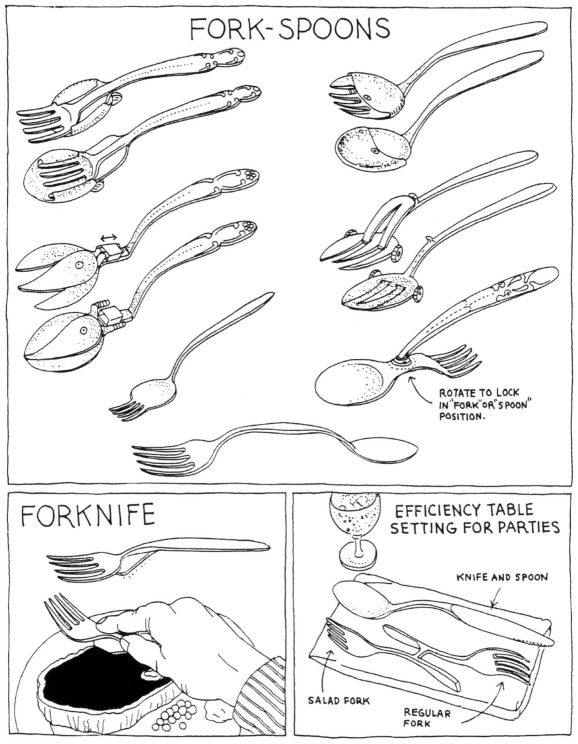

FORK-SPOONS

ROTATE TO LOCK IN "FORK" OR "SPOON" POSITION.

FORKNIFE

EFFICIENCY TABLE SETTING FOR PARTIES

KNIFE AND SPOON

SALAD FORK

REGULAR FORK

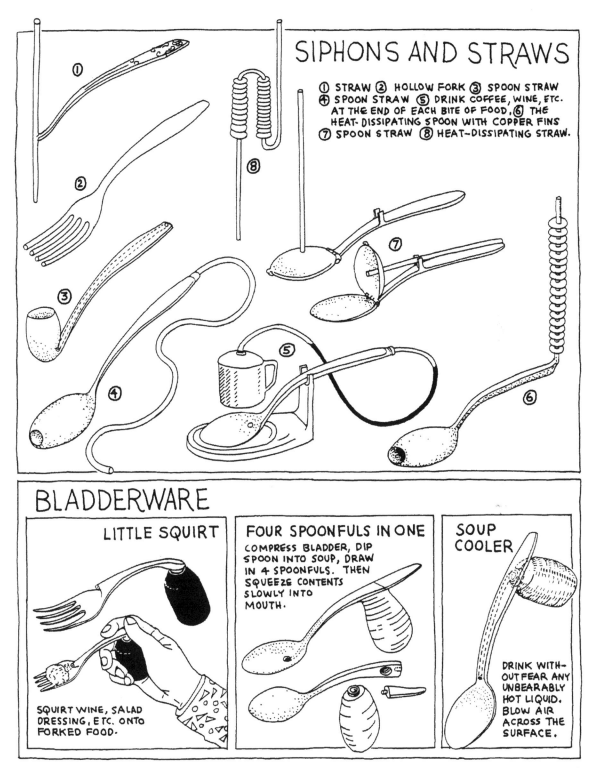

SIPHONS AND STRAWS

① STRAW ② HOLLOW FORK ③ SPOON STRAW
④ SPOON STRAW ⑤ DRINK COFFEE, WINE, ETC.
AT THE END OF EACH BITE OF FOOD, ⑥ THE
HEAT-DISSIPATING SPOON WITH COPPER FINS
⑦ SPOON STRAW ⑧ HEAT-DISSIPATING STRAW.

BLADDERWARE

LITTLE SQUIRT

SQUIRT WINE, SALAD
DRESSING, ETC. ONTO
FORKED FOOD.

FOUR SPOONFULS IN ONE

COMPRESS BLADDER, DIP
SPOON INTO SOUP, DRAW
IN 4 SPOONFULS. THEN
SQUEEZE CONTENTS
SLOWLY INTO
MOUTH.

SOUP COOLER

DRINK WITH-
OUT FEAR ANY
UNBEARABLY
HOT LIQUID.
BLOW AIR
ACROSS THE
SURFACE.

COMMUTERS' BREAKFAST KIT

THIS KIT IS THE IDEAL THING FOR CAPITALIZING ON "LOST" FREEWAY COMMUTING TIME. EAT, DRINK SAFELY WITH YOUR EYES ON THE ROAD. KIT CONTAINS: SCREW-TOP LIDS, SIPPER UNIT (*SEE INSET*), BIB, NECKSTRAP, UTENSILS AND NAPKINS.

NECKSTRAP

BIB

ACCESSORY SIPPER UNIT FOR COFFEE, OTHER DRINKS.

DRINKING WHILE DRIVING

NON-ALCOHOLIC BEVERAGES CAN BE SAFELY SIPPED WITHOUT SPILLING.

DRINK 'N DRIVE

BASE UNIT IS AF-FIXED TO DASH-BOARD. INSULATED CUP IS REMOVABLE.

"SIPSTRAP"

OFFICE FURNISHINGS AND SUPPLIES

THE STAPLER

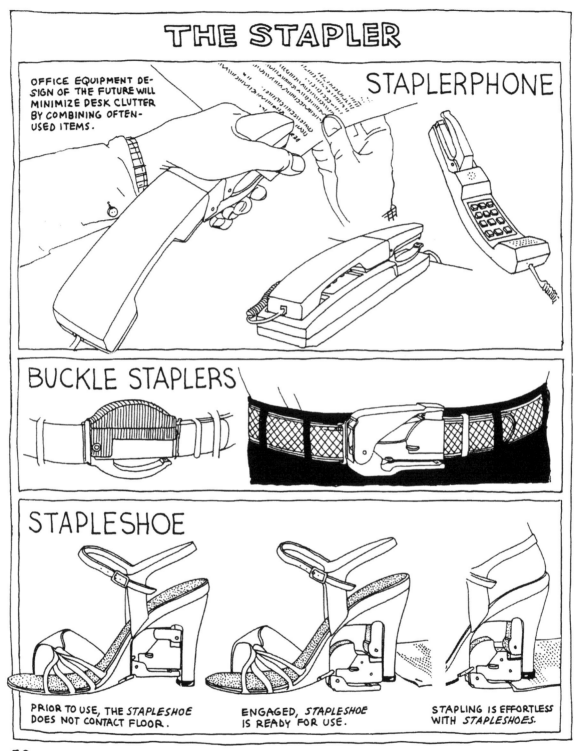

OFFICE EQUIPMENT DESIGN OF THE FUTURE WILL MINIMIZE DESK CLUTTER BY COMBINING OFTEN-USED ITEMS.

STAPLERPHONE

BUCKLE STAPLERS

STAPLESHOE

PRIOR TO USE, THE *STAPLESHOE* DOES NOT CONTACT FLOOR.

ENGAGED, *STAPLESHOE* IS READY FOR USE.

STAPLING IS EFFORTLESS WITH *STAPLESHOES.*

THE PERISCOPE VDT
(VIDEO DISPLAY TERMINAL)

WIDESPREAD ADOPTION OF THE VDT FOR OFFICE USE HAS BEEN AC-COMPANIED BY USER COMPLAINTS OF EYESTRAIN, HEADACHES, AND AN ABNORMAL RATE OF MISCARRIAGES. PREGNANT WOMEN, AND INDEED ALL OTHERS WHO FEAR RADIATION LEAKAGE, WILL APPRECI-IATE THE *PERISCOPE VDT*. THE TERMINAL IS 4'-8' FROM USER, DE-PENDING ON WHICH MODEL IS CHOSEN.

A ROOMFUL OF VDTS CAN BE DE-SIGNED WITH HORIZONTAL PERI-SCOPES CONNECTED TO TERMINALS BEHIND A LEAD-LINED WALL.

BOOKCASES

TERMINALS

VDT — MIRROR

A PAIR OF PARALLEL MIRRORS, FIXED AT 45°, GIVES A CLEAR VIEW OF THE VDT WHICH IS LOCATED NEAR THE CEILING. A MAGNIFYING LENS COMPENSATES FOR THE REDUCED IMAGE SIZE.

KEYBOARD

MIRROR

OFFICE CHAIRS

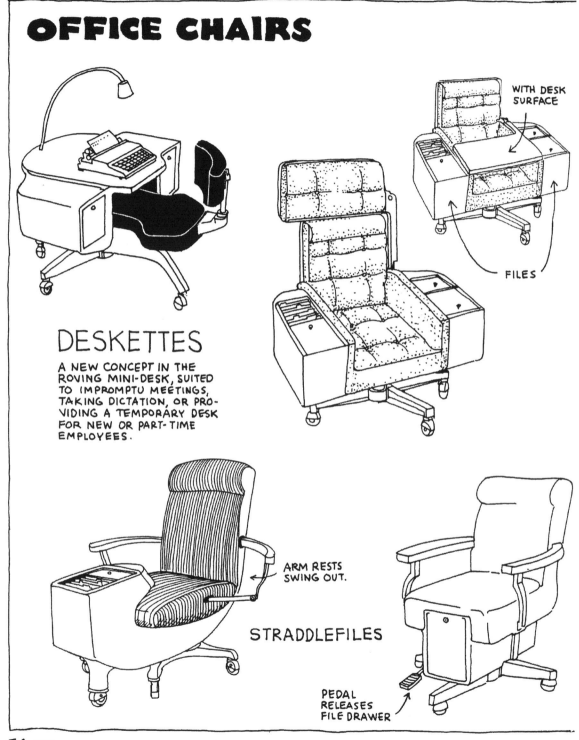

WITH DESK
SURFACE

FILES

DESKETTES

A NEW CONCEPT IN THE
ROVING MINI-DESK, SUITED
TO IMPROMPTU MEETINGS,
TAKING DICTATION, OR PRO-
VIDING A TEMPORARY DESK
FOR NEW OR PART-TIME
EMPLOYEES.

ARM RESTS
SWING OUT.

STRADDLEFILES

PEDAL
RELEASES
FILE DRAWER

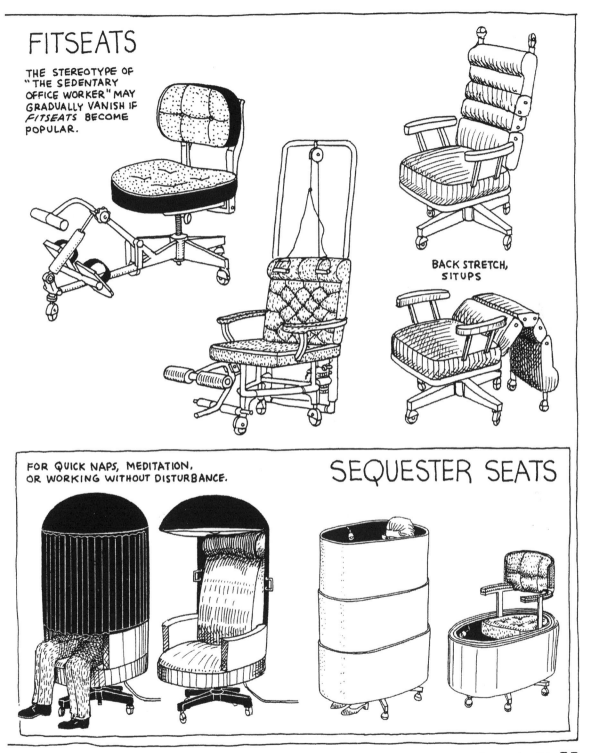

FITSEATS

THE STEREOTYPE OF "THE SEDENTARY OFFICE WORKER" MAY GRADUALLY VANISH IF *FITSEATS* BECOME POPULAR.

BACK STRETCH, SITUPS

SEQUESTER SEATS

FOR QUICK NAPS, MEDITATION, OR WORKING WITHOUT DISTURBANCE.

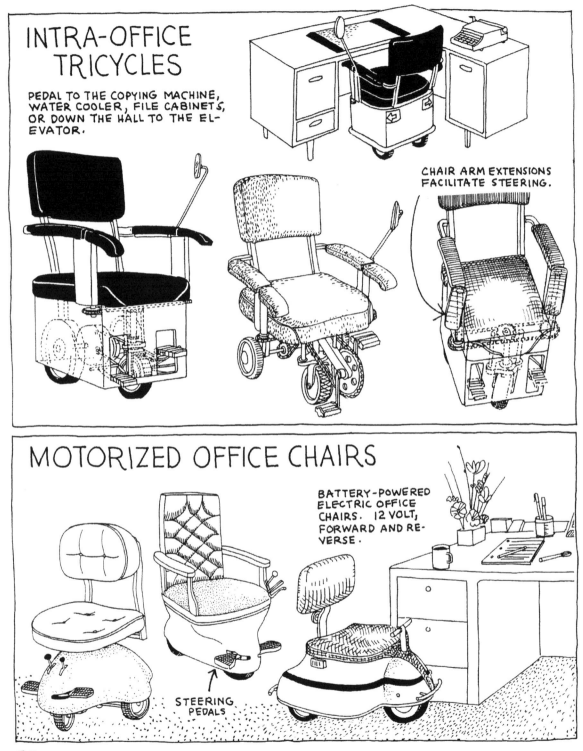

INTRA-OFFICE TRICYCLES

PEDAL TO THE COPYING MACHINE, WATER COOLER, FILE CABINETS, OR DOWN THE HALL TO THE ELEVATOR.

CHAIR ARM EXTENSIONS FACILITATE STEERING.

MOTORIZED OFFICE CHAIRS

BATTERY-POWERED ELECTRIC OFFICE CHAIRS. 12 VOLT, FORWARD AND REVERSE.

STEERING PEDALS

MOTORCYCLE OFFICE
(ON A NICE DAY, TAKE THE OFFICE OUTDOORS)

- DRAFTING CHAIR ROTATES 180° FOR ACCESS TO REAR DRAFTING DESK.
- LOCKING DESK DRAWERS
- DESK LEGS WITHDRAW DURING TRAVEL.

WINDSHIELD FOLDS FOR AERODYNAMIC EFFICIENCY.

LK539

BENCH PRESS DESK

MODERN OFFICES INCREASINGLY OFFER FITNESS PROGRAMS, EXERCISE BREAKS AS WELL AS ON-SITE FACILITIES SUCH AS SAUNAS, WEIGHT ROOMS AND SWIMMING POOLS FOR THE NEW FITNESS-CONSCIOUS EMPLOYEE. SMART EMPLOYERS WILL PROVIDE A BENCH PRESS DESK FOR THE MAN OR WOMAN WHO LACKS TIME TO GO TO THE WEIGHT ROOM.

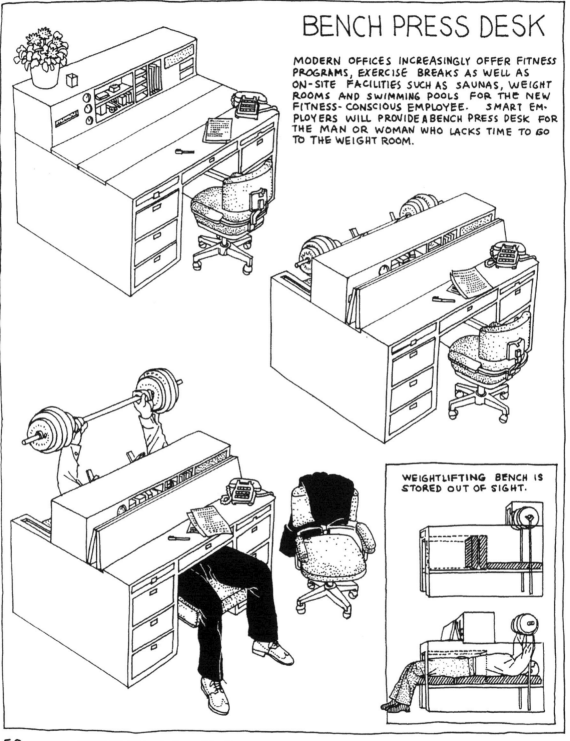

WEIGHTLIFTING BENCH IS STORED OUT OF SIGHT.

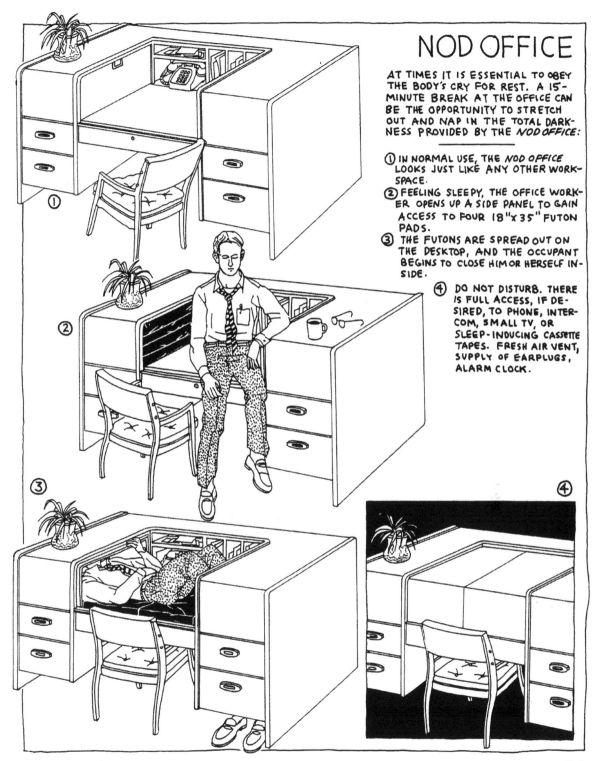

NOD OFFICE

AT TIMES IT IS ESSENTIAL TO OBEY THE BODY'S CRY FOR REST. A 15-MINUTE BREAK AT THE OFFICE CAN BE THE OPPORTUNITY TO STRETCH OUT AND NAP IN THE TOTAL DARKNESS PROVIDED BY THE *NOD OFFICE*:

1. IN NORMAL USE, THE *NOD OFFICE* LOOKS JUST LIKE ANY OTHER WORKSPACE.
2. FEELING SLEEPY, THE OFFICE WORKER OPENS UP A SIDE PANEL TO GAIN ACCESS TO FOUR 18"x35" FUTON PADS.
3. THE FUTONS ARE SPREAD OUT ON THE DESKTOP, AND THE OCCUPANT BEGINS TO CLOSE HIM OR HERSELF INSIDE.
4. DO NOT DISTURB. THERE IS FULL ACCESS, IF DESIRED, TO PHONE, INTERCOM, SMALL TV, OR SLEEP-INDUCING CASSETTE TAPES. FRESH AIR VENT, SUPPLY OF EARPLUGS, ALARM CLOCK.

OFFICE FURNISHINGS AND SUPPLIES 59

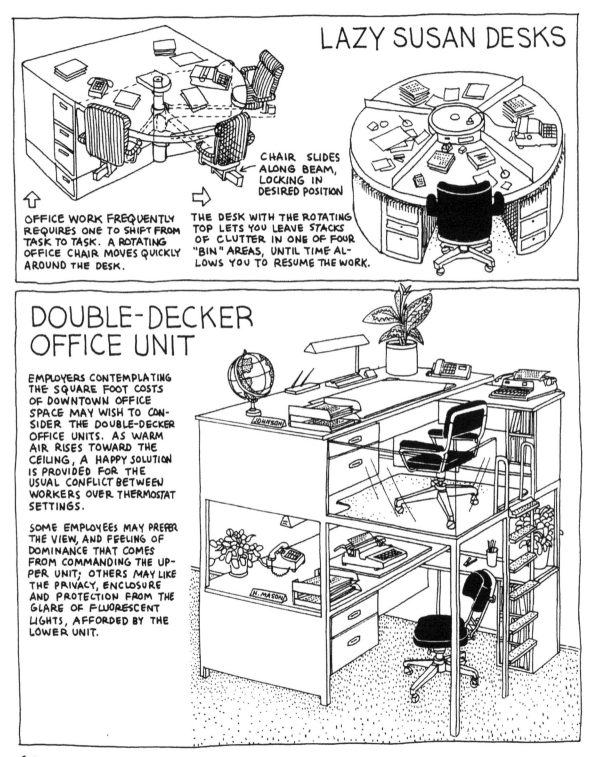

LAZY SUSAN DESKS

⬆ OFFICE WORK FREQUENTLY REQUIRES ONE TO SHIFT FROM TASK TO TASK. A ROTATING OFFICE CHAIR MOVES QUICKLY AROUND THE DESK.

⮕ THE DESK WITH THE ROTATING TOP LETS YOU LEAVE STACKS OF CLUTTER IN ONE OF FOUR "BIN" AREAS, UNTIL TIME ALLOWS YOU TO RESUME THE WORK.

CHAIR SLIDES ALONG BEAM, LOCKING IN DESIRED POSITION

DOUBLE-DECKER OFFICE UNIT

EMPLOYERS CONTEMPLATING THE SQUARE FOOT COSTS OF DOWNTOWN OFFICE SPACE MAY WISH TO CONSIDER THE DOUBLE-DECKER OFFICE UNITS. AS WARM AIR RISES TOWARD THE CEILING, A HAPPY SOLUTION IS PROVIDED FOR THE USUAL CONFLICT BETWEEN WORKERS OVER THERMOSTAT SETTINGS.

SOME EMPLOYEES MAY PREFER THE VIEW, AND FEELING OF DOMINANCE THAT COMES FROM COMMANDING THE UPPER UNIT; OTHERS MAY LIKE THE PRIVACY, ENCLOSURE AND PROTECTION FROM THE GLARE OF FLUORESCENT LIGHTS, AFFORDED BY THE LOWER UNIT.

HOME FURNISHINGS AND APPLIANCES

FURNITURE WITH MANY FACES

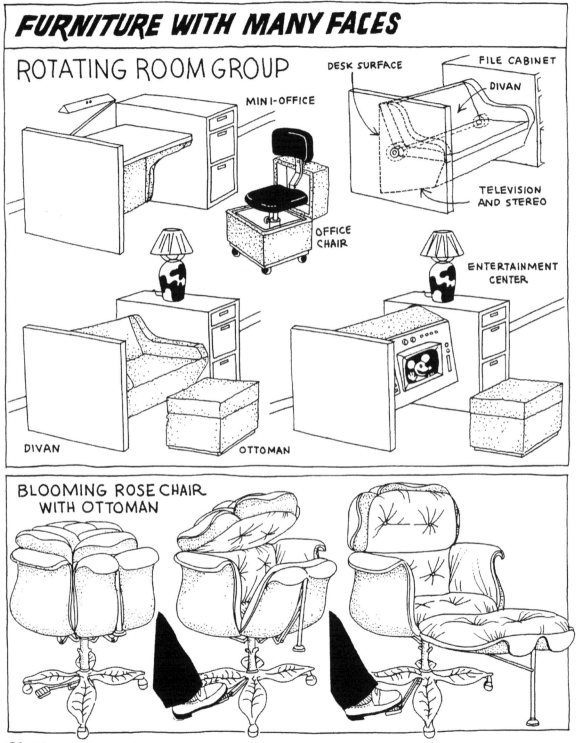

ROTATING ROOM GROUP

DESK SURFACE

FILE CABINET

DIVAN

MINI-OFFICE

OFFICE CHAIR

TELEVISION AND STEREO

ENTERTAINMENT CENTER

DIVAN

OTTOMAN

BLOOMING ROSE CHAIR WITH OTTOMAN

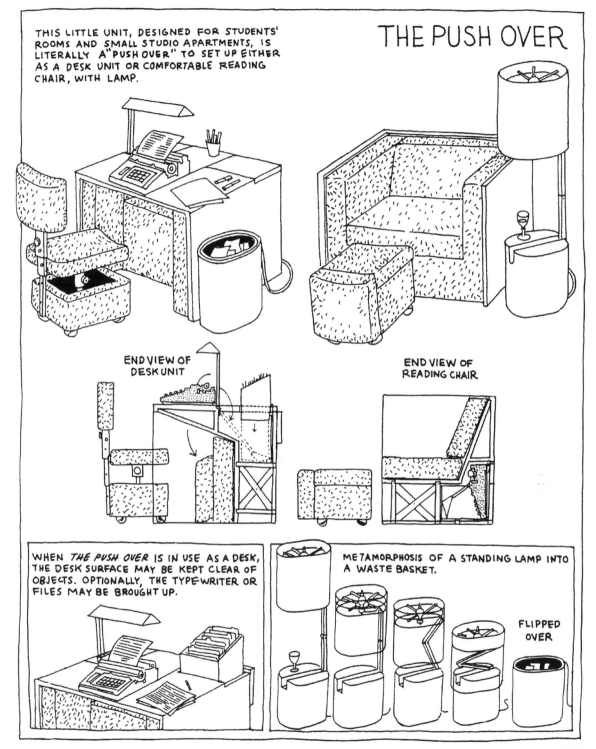

THIS LITTLE UNIT, DESIGNED FOR STUDENTS' ROOMS AND SMALL STUDIO APARTMENTS, IS LITERALLY A "PUSH OVER" TO SET UP EITHER AS A DESK UNIT OR COMFORTABLE READING CHAIR, WITH LAMP.

THE PUSH OVER

END VIEW OF DESK UNIT

END VIEW OF READING CHAIR

WHEN *THE PUSH OVER* IS IN USE AS A DESK, THE DESK SURFACE MAY BE KEPT CLEAR OF OBJECTS. OPTIONALLY, THE TYPEWRITER OR FILES MAY BE BROUGHT UP.

METAMORPHOSIS OF A STANDING LAMP INTO A WASTE BASKET.

FLIPPED OVER

FURNITURE FOR HIGH-LEVEL CONVERSATIONS

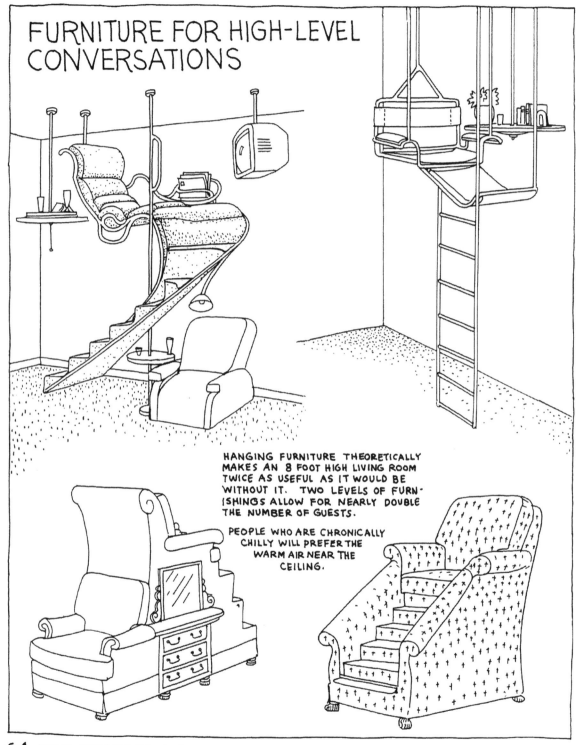

HANGING FURNITURE THEORETICALLY MAKES AN 8 FOOT HIGH LIVING ROOM TWICE AS USEFUL AS IT WOULD BE WITHOUT IT. TWO LEVELS OF FURNISHINGS ALLOW FOR NEARLY DOUBLE THE NUMBER OF GUESTS.

PEOPLE WHO ARE CHRONICALLY CHILLY WILL PREFER THE WARM AIR NEAR THE CEILING.

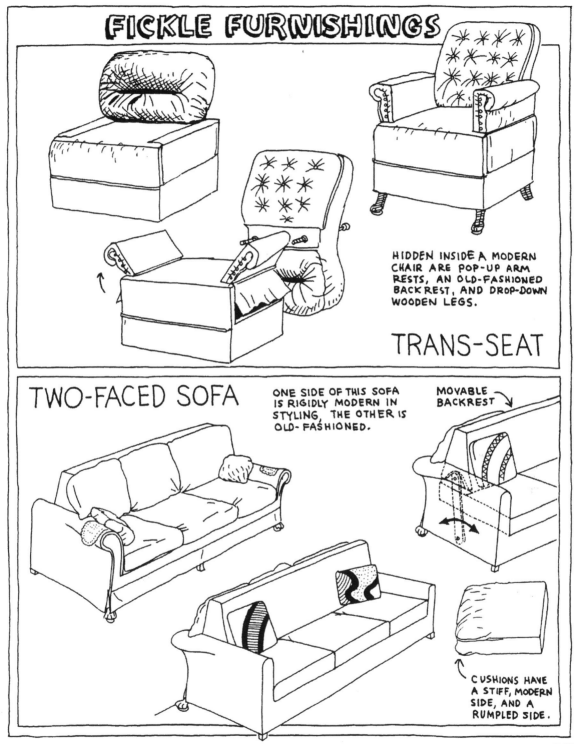

FICKLE FURNISHINGS

HIDDEN INSIDE A MODERN CHAIR ARE POP-UP ARM RESTS, AN OLD-FASHIONED BACK REST, AND DROP-DOWN WOODEN LEGS.

TRANS-SEAT

TWO-FACED SOFA

ONE SIDE OF THIS SOFA IS RIGIDLY MODERN IN STYLING, THE OTHER IS OLD-FASHIONED.

MOVABLE BACKREST

CUSHIONS HAVE A STIFF, MODERN SIDE, AND A RUMPLED SIDE.

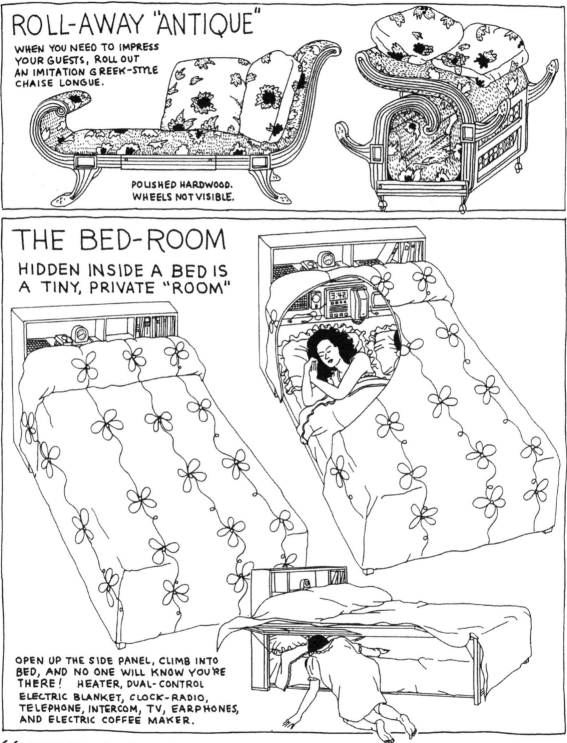

ROLL-AWAY "ANTIQUE"

WHEN YOU NEED TO IMPRESS
YOUR GUESTS, ROLL OUT
AN IMITATION GREEK-STYLE
CHAISE LONGUE.

POLISHED HARDWOOD.
WHEELS NOT VISIBLE.

THE BED-ROOM

HIDDEN INSIDE A BED IS
A TINY, PRIVATE "ROOM"

OPEN UP THE SIDE PANEL, CLIMB INTO
BED, AND NO ONE WILL KNOW YOU'RE
THERE! HEATER, DUAL-CONTROL
ELECTRIC BLANKET, CLOCK-RADIO,
TELEPHONE, INTERCOM, TV, EARPHONES,
AND ELECTRIC COFFEE MAKER.

MILDLY THERAPEUTIC FURNITURE

ELDERLY COUPLES, ESPECIALLY, WILL APPRECIATE THESE CONSERVATIVELY STYLED FURNISHINGS ADAPTED TO MEET THE NEEDS OF THE 80's FITNESS CRAZE.

LIVING ROOM TEETER-TOTTER

TWO-PERSON ROCKING CHAIR

THOUGH SOMEWHAT BIZARRE IN APPEARANCE, THIS NOVEL DINING ROOM PIECE IS AN EXCELLENT MASSAGE TABLE.

WORKOUT FURNITURE

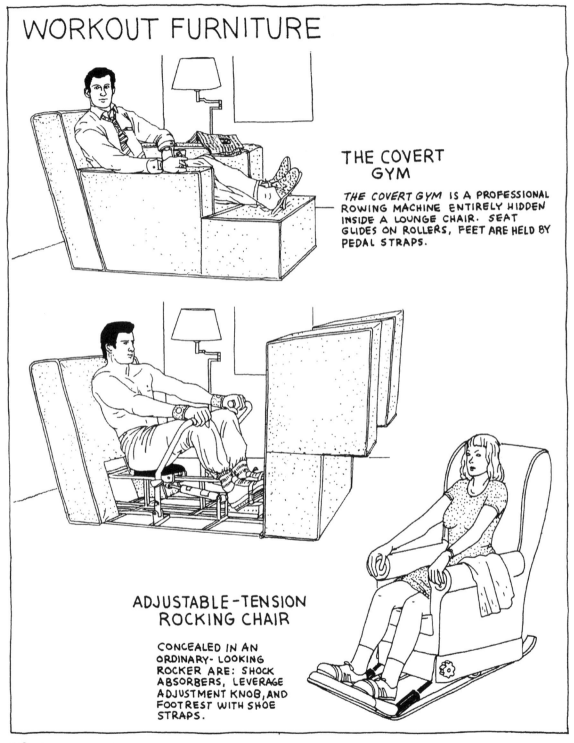

THE COVERT GYM

THE COVERT GYM IS A PROFESSIONAL ROWING MACHINE ENTIRELY HIDDEN INSIDE A LOUNGE CHAIR. SEAT GLIDES ON ROLLERS, FEET ARE HELD BY PEDAL STRAPS.

ADJUSTABLE-TENSION ROCKING CHAIR

CONCEALED *IN AN ORDINARY- LOOKING ROCKER ARE:* SHOCK ABSORBERS, LEVERAGE ADJUSTMENT KNOB, AND FOOTREST WITH SHOE STRAPS.

3-POSITION INCLINER

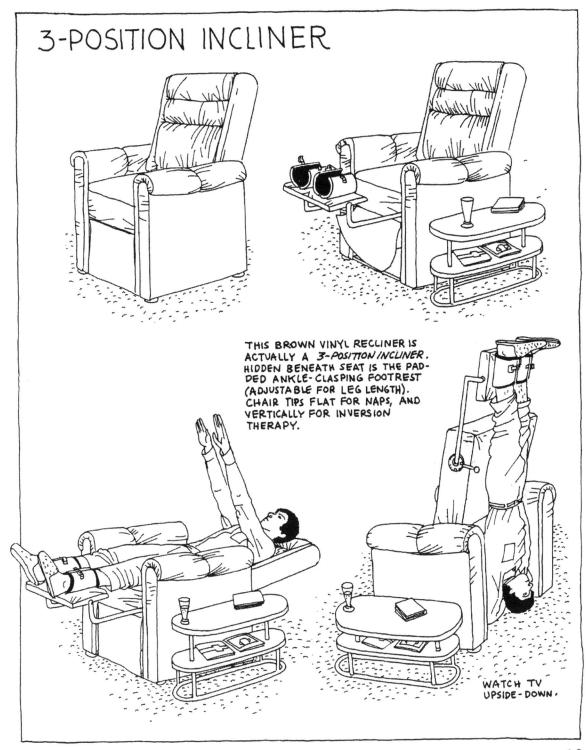

THIS BROWN VINYL RECLINER IS
ACTUALLY A *3-POSITION INCLINER.*
HIDDEN BENEATH SEAT IS THE PAD-
DED ANKLE-CLASPING FOOTREST
(ADJUSTABLE FOR LEG LENGTH).
CHAIR TIPS FLAT FOR NAPS, AND
VERTICALLY FOR INVERSION
THERAPY.

WATCH TV
UPSIDE-DOWN.

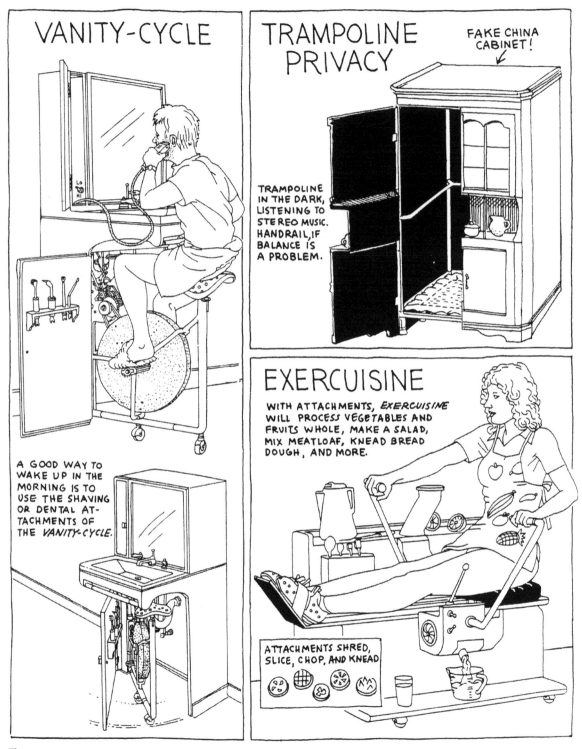

VANITY-CYCLE

A GOOD WAY TO WAKE UP IN THE MORNING IS TO USE THE SHAVING OR DENTAL ATTACHMENTS OF THE *VANITY-CYCLE*.

TRAMPOLINE PRIVACY

FAKE CHINA CABINET!

TRAMPOLINE IN THE DARK, LISTENING TO STEREO MUSIC. HANDRAIL, IF BALANCE IS A PROBLEM.

EXERCUISINE

WITH ATTACHMENTS, *EXERCUISINE* WILL PROCESS VEGETABLES AND FRUITS WHOLE, MAKE A SALAD, MIX MEATLOAF, KNEAD BREAD DOUGH, AND MORE.

ATTACHMENTS SHRED, SLICE, CHOP, AND KNEAD

VACUUMING FOR HEALTH

VACUUM SUIT

WEARING THE *VACUUM SUIT*, ONE FEELS FREE TO MOVE AROUND THE HOUSE, DEVELOPING A SKATING OR DANCING MOTION WHILE LISTENING TO STEREO HEADPHONES. VACUUM MOTOR CAN BE REVERSED FOR YARD LEAF BLOWING. "SAUNA" SUIT HELPS ONE TO LOSE WEIGHT.

50 FT. GROUNDED ELECTRICAL CORD

KNEE SWEEPS

EXERVAC

LEVER DISENGAGES VACUUM AND ENGAGES WHEELS FOR FORWARD OR REVERSE.

TWO SPEEDS

SWEEP SHOES

SCOOTING AROUND THE HOUSE DOING OTHER CHORES, YOU WILL FORGET YOU HAVE THESE ON!

WASHING MACHINE SPA

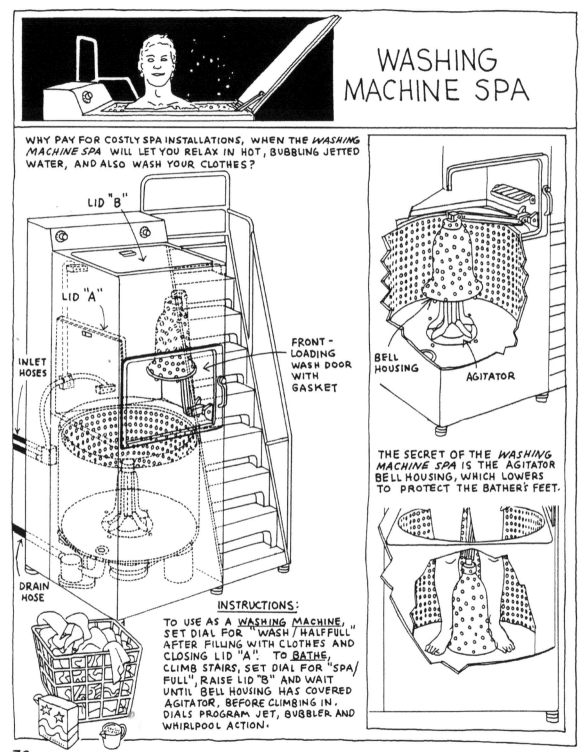

WHY PAY FOR COSTLY SPA INSTALLATIONS, WHEN THE *WASHING MACHINE SPA* WILL LET YOU RELAX IN HOT, BUBBLING JETTED WATER, AND ALSO WASH YOUR CLOTHES?

LID "B"

LID "A"

INLET HOSES

FRONT - LOADING WASH DOOR WITH GASKET

DRAIN HOSE

BELL HOUSING

AGITATOR

THE SECRET OF THE *WASHING MACHINE SPA* IS THE AGITATOR BELL HOUSING, WHICH LOWERS TO PROTECT THE BATHER'S FEET.

INSTRUCTIONS:

TO USE AS A <u>WASHING MACHINE,</u> SET DIAL FOR "WASH / HALFFULL" AFTER FILLING WITH CLOTHES AND CLOSING LID "A". TO <u>BATHE,</u> CLIMB STAIRS, SET DIAL FOR "SPA/ FULL", RAISE LID "B" AND WAIT UNTIL BELL HOUSING HAS COVERED AGITATOR, BEFORE CLIMBING IN. DIALS PROGRAM JET, BUBBLER AND WHIRLPOOL ACTION.

THE BATHROOM

INTEGRAL, SPACE-CONSERVING FIXTURES

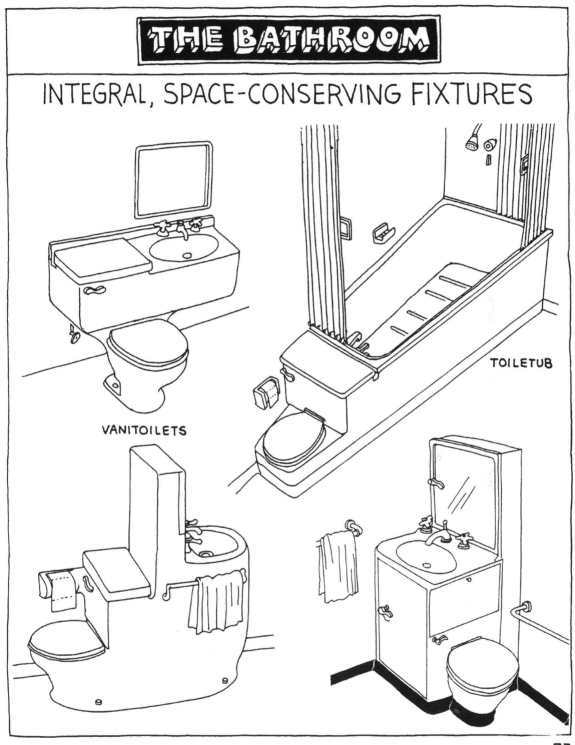

VANITOILETS

TOILETUB

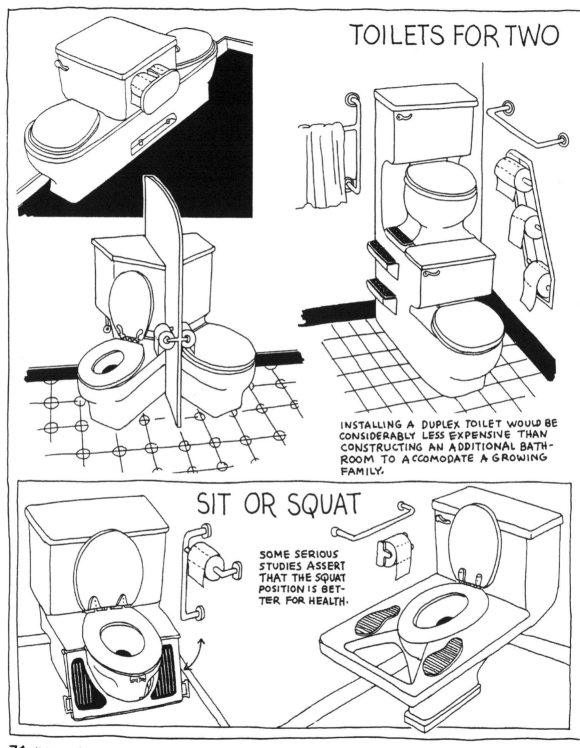

TOILETS FOR TWO

INSTALLING A DUPLEX TOILET WOULD BE CONSIDERABLY LESS EXPENSIVE THAN CONSTRUCTING AN ADDITIONAL BATHROOM TO ACCOMODATE A GROWING FAMILY.

SIT OR SQUAT

SOME SERIOUS STUDIES ASSERT THAT THE SQUAT POSITION IS BETTER FOR HEALTH.

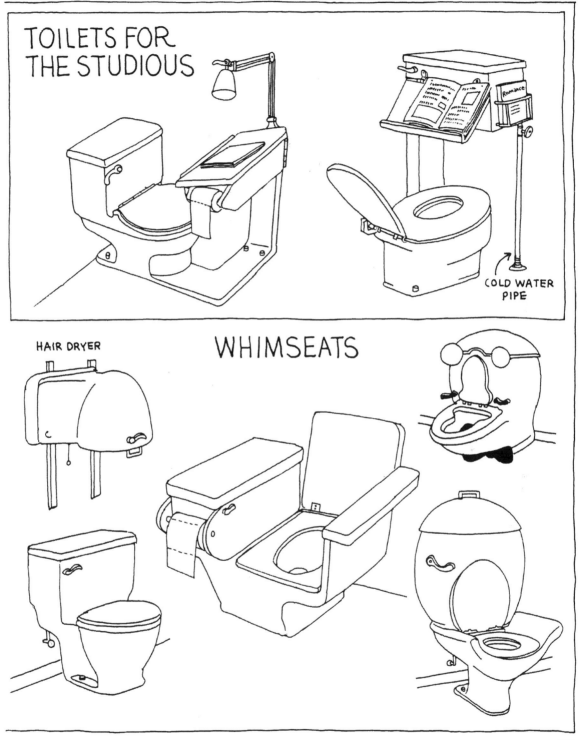

TOILETS FOR
THE STUDIOUS

COLD WATER
PIPE

HAIR DRYER

WHIMSEATS

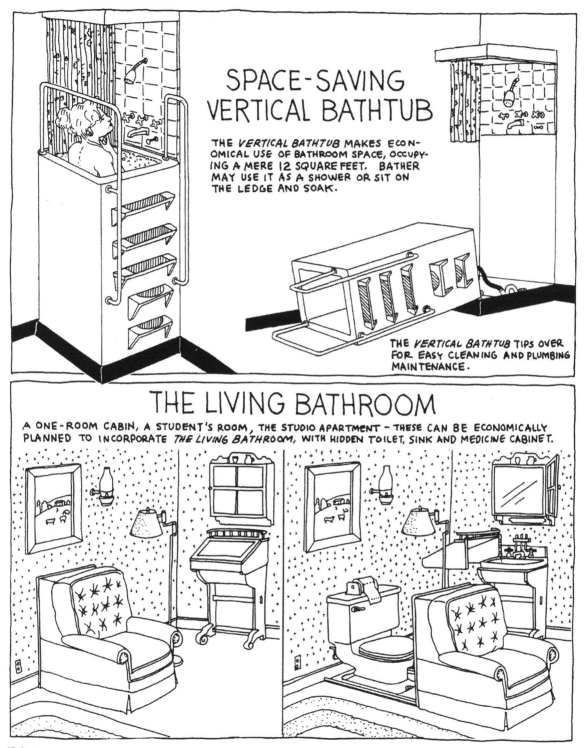

SPACE-SAVING VERTICAL BATHTUB

THE *VERTICAL BATHTUB* MAKES ECON-
OMICAL USE OF BATHROOM SPACE, OCCUPY-
ING A MERE 12 SQUARE FEET. BATHER
MAY USE IT AS A SHOWER OR SIT ON
THE LEDGE AND SOAK.

THE *VERTICAL BATHTUB* TIPS OVER
FOR EASY CLEANING AND PLUMBING
MAINTENANCE.

THE LIVING BATHROOM

A ONE-ROOM CABIN, A STUDENT'S ROOM, THE STUDIO APARTMENT — THESE CAN BE ECONOMICALLY
PLANNED TO INCORPORATE *THE LIVING BATHROOM*, WITH HIDDEN TOILET, SINK AND MEDICINE CABINET.

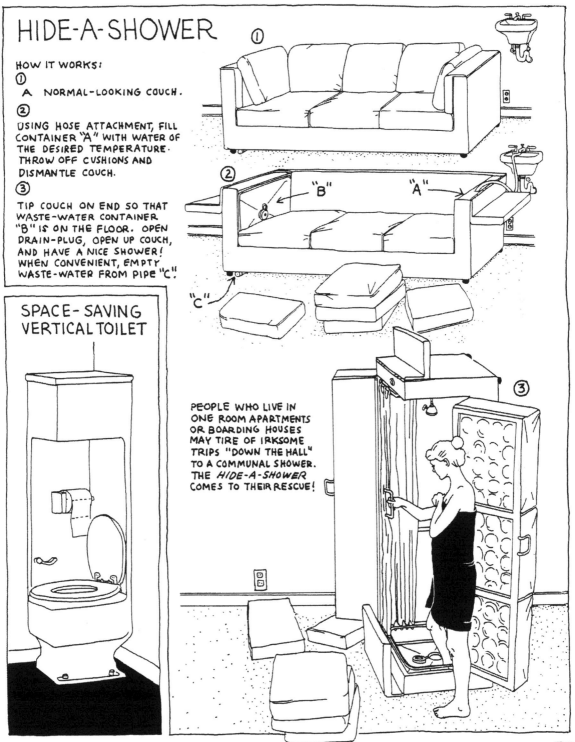

HIDE-A-SHOWER

HOW IT WORKS:

① A NORMAL-LOOKING COUCH.

② USING HOSE ATTACHMENT, FILL CONTAINER "A" WITH WATER OF THE DESIRED TEMPERATURE. THROW OFF CUSHIONS AND DISMANTLE COUCH.

③ TIP COUCH ON END SO THAT WASTE-WATER CONTAINER "B" IS ON THE FLOOR. OPEN DRAIN-PLUG, OPEN UP COUCH, AND HAVE A NICE SHOWER! WHEN CONVENIENT, EMPTY WASTE-WATER FROM PIPE "C".

SPACE-SAVING VERTICAL TOILET

PEOPLE WHO LIVE IN ONE ROOM APARTMENTS OR BOARDING HOUSES MAY TIRE OF IRKSOME TRIPS "DOWN THE HALL" TO A COMMUNAL SHOWER. THE *HIDE-A-SHOWER* COMES TO THEIR RESCUE!

HOME WASTE MANAGEMENT

MANUAL GARBAGE DISPOSAL

ONE WAY TO MANIFEST YOUR INDEPENDENCE FROM THE ELECTRIC COMPANY IS TO INSTALL A MANUAL GARBAGE DISPOSAL. IT WILL TAKE PRACTICE AT FIRST TO GET INTO THE RHYTHM OF PULLING THE FLYWHEEL PULL-ROPE, WHILE STUFFING GARBAGE DOWN THE DRAIN. IT IS EXCELLENT EXERCISE.

THIS DISPOSAL UNIT CONSISTS OF A HEAVY FLY-WHEEL MOUNTED ON A SHAFT IN THE PLACE OF AN ELECTRIC MOTOR. THE FLYWHEEL PULL-ROPE IS DE-SIGNED WITH A SPRING RECOIL FEATURE.

NOTE:
CHECK RPM GAUGE FOR PROPER FLYWHEEL SPEED FOR ICE, BONE AND OTHER HARD THINGS.

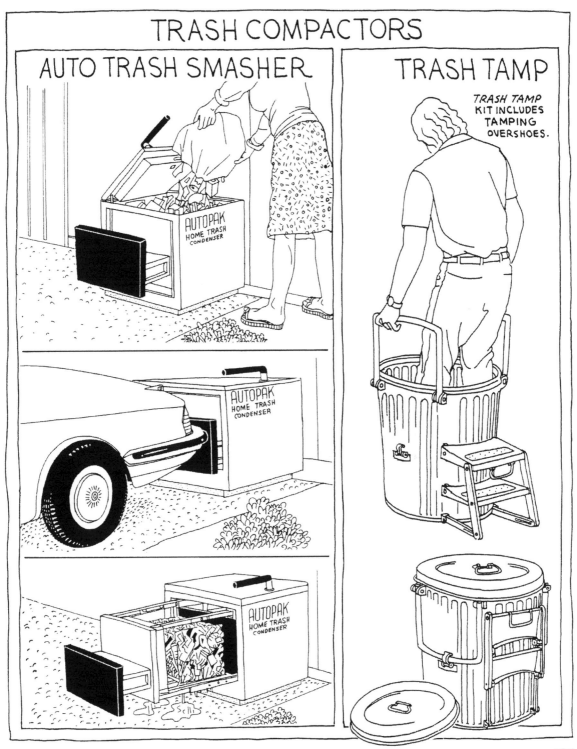

TRASH COMPACTORS

AUTO TRASH SMASHER

TRASH TAMP

TRASH TAMP KIT INCLUDES TAMPING OVERSHOES.

AUTOPAK HOME TRASH CONDENSER

AUTOPAK HOME TRASH CONDENSER

AUTOPAK HOME TRASH CONDENSER

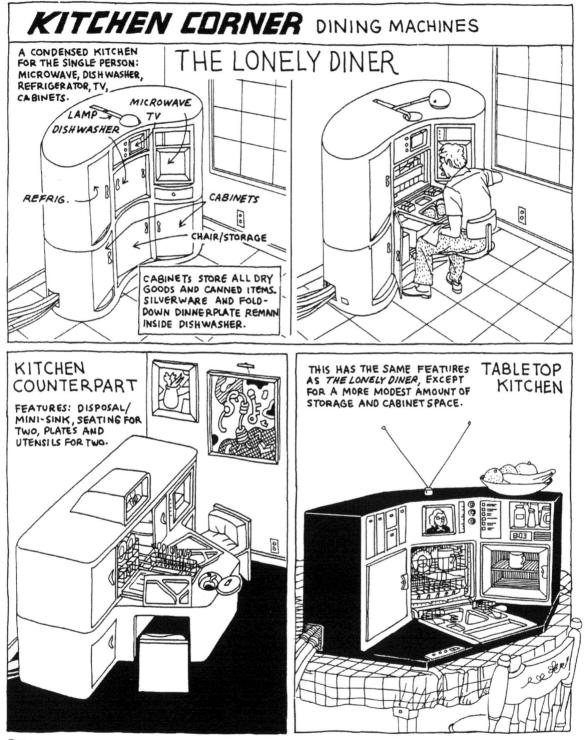

KITCHEN CORNER DINING MACHINES

THE LONELY DINER

A CONDENSED KITCHEN FOR THE SINGLE PERSON: MICROWAVE, DISHWASHER, REFRIGERATOR, TV, CABINETS.

LAMP
MICROWAVE
TV
DISHWASHER
REFRIG.
CABINETS
CHAIR/STORAGE

CABINETS STORE ALL DRY GOODS AND CANNED ITEMS. SILVERWARE AND FOLD-DOWN DINNERPLATE REMAIN INSIDE DISHWASHER.

KITCHEN COUNTERPART

FEATURES: DISPOSAL/ MINI-SINK, SEATING FOR TWO, PLATES AND UTENSILS FOR TWO.

TABLETOP KITCHEN

THIS HAS THE SAME FEATURES AS *THE LONELY DINER*, EXCEPT FOR A MORE MODEST AMOUNT OF STORAGE AND CABINET SPACE.

GARDENING GADGETS

GARDEN IMPLEMENTS

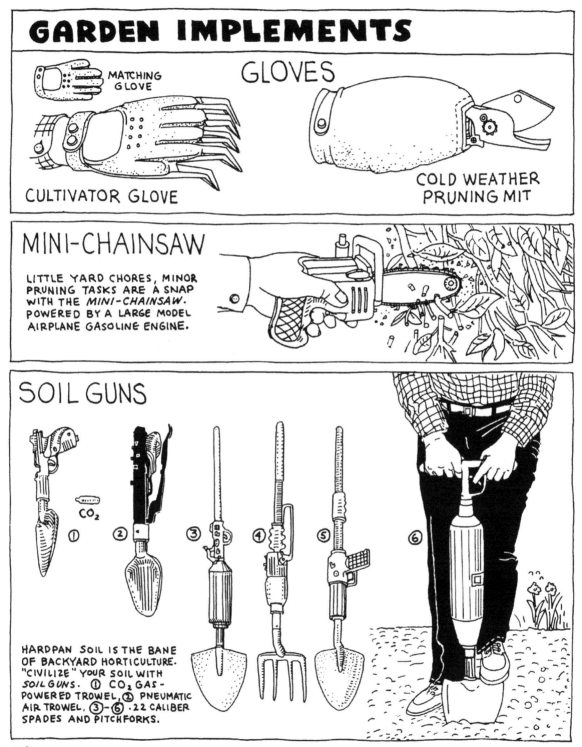

GLOVES

MATCHING GLOVE

CULTIVATOR GLOVE

COLD WEATHER PRUNING MIT

MINI-CHAINSAW

LITTLE YARD CHORES, MINOR PRUNING TASKS ARE A SNAP WITH THE *MINI-CHAINSAW.* POWERED BY A LARGE MODEL AIRPLANE GASOLINE ENGINE.

SOIL GUNS

CO₂

① ② ③ ④ ⑤ ⑥

HARDPAN SOIL IS THE BANE OF BACKYARD HORTICULTURE. "CIVILIZE" YOUR SOIL WITH *SOIL GUNS.* ① CO₂ GAS-POWERED TROWEL, ② PNEUMATIC AIR TROWEL, ③-⑥ .22 CALIBER SPADES AND PITCHFORKS.

GARDENING SHOES

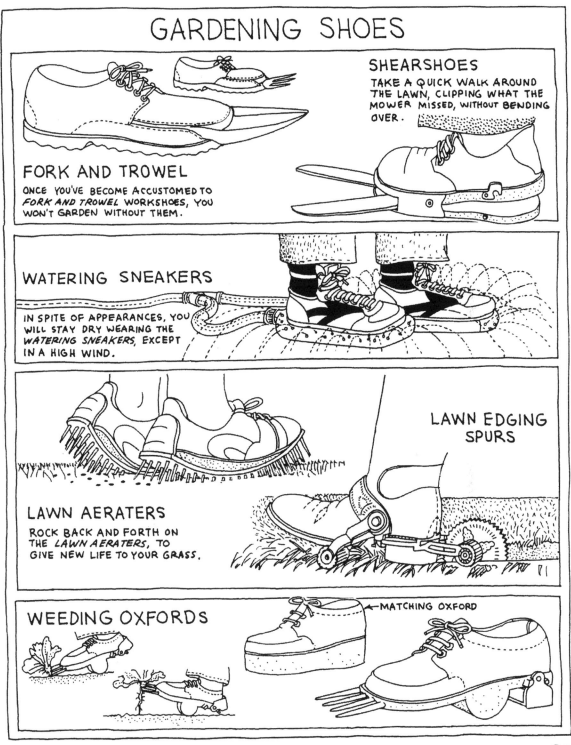

SHEARSHOES
TAKE A QUICK WALK AROUND THE LAWN, CLIPPING WHAT THE MOWER MISSED, WITHOUT BENDING OVER.

FORK AND TROWEL
ONCE YOU'VE BECOME ACCUSTOMED TO *FORK AND TROWEL* WORKSHOES, YOU WON'T GARDEN WITHOUT THEM.

WATERING SNEAKERS
IN SPITE OF APPEARANCES, YOU WILL STAY DRY WEARING THE *WATERING SNEAKERS*, EXCEPT IN A HIGH WIND.

LAWN EDGING SPURS

LAWN AERATERS
ROCK BACK AND FORTH ON THE *LAWN AERATERS*, TO GIVE NEW LIFE TO YOUR GRASS.

WEEDING OXFORDS

←MATCHING OXFORD

POWER LAWN MOWERS

RIDING MOWERS FOR SMALL LAWNS

MOWERCYCLES

LAWNBUG

MULCHING STROLLER

THE TENDER BEHIND

MOWERPED

UNDER AVERAGE CONDITIONS, IT IS NOT NECESSARY FOR THE RIDER OF THE *MOWERPED* TO PEDAL, BUT IN TALL GRASS OR ON SLOPES, THE ENGINE NEEDS HELP.

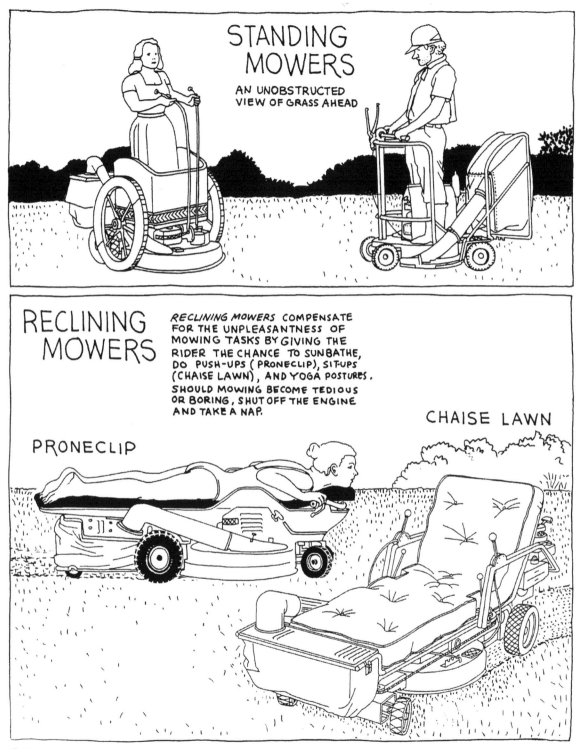

STANDING MOWERS

AN UNOBSTRUCTED VIEW OF GRASS AHEAD

RECLINING MOWERS

RECLINING MOWERS COMPENSATE FOR THE UNPLEASANTNESS OF MOWING TASKS BY GIVING THE RIDER THE CHANCE TO SUNBATHE, DO PUSH-UPS (PRONECLIP), SIT-UPS (CHAISE LAWN), AND YOGA POSTURES. SHOULD MOWING BECOME TEDIOUS OR BORING, SHUT OFF THE ENGINE AND TAKE A NAP.

PRONECLIP

CHAISE LAWN

CAMPING AND SURVIVAL GEAR

BACKPACKS

INTERNAL FRAME DROLLPACKS

INTERNAL FRAME DROLL PACKS ARE DESIGNED FOR BALANCE AND VERSATILITY, AS WELL AS FOR HELPING THE HIKER MAINTAIN A CHEERFUL ATTITUDE.

RACSACK

BUGPACKS

BUGPACKS ARE INTERNAL FRAME BACKPACKS DESIGNED PRINCIPALLY FOR USE BY ENTOMOLOGISTS ON FIELDTRIPS. THESE ARE TRUE EXPEDITION PACKS AS WELL AS RUCKSACKS FOR TECHNICAL CLIMBING.

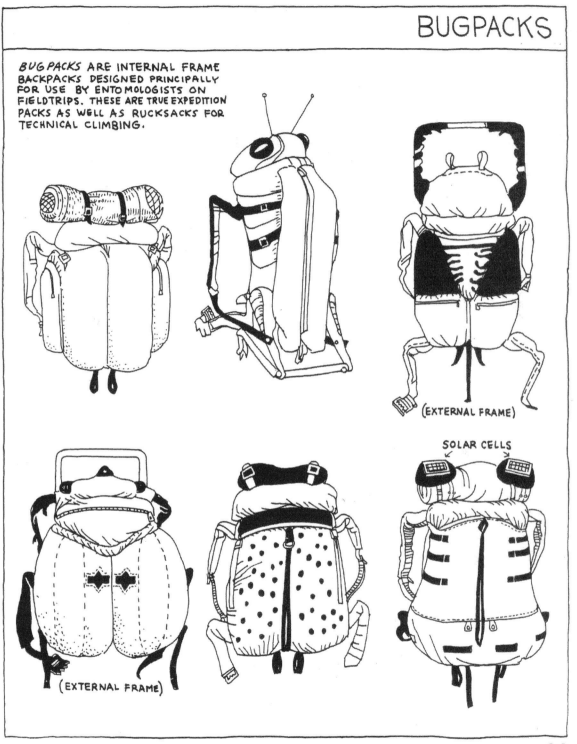

(EXTERNAL FRAME)

(EXTERNAL FRAME)

SOLAR CELLS

MUGSACKS

THE PRESIDENT SERIES

BACKPACK HOTEL

IF YOU DON'T MIND SLEEP- IN A SITTING POSTURE, THE *BACKPACK HOTEL* IS THE PERFECT EMERGENCY BIVOUAC SACK. WHEN YOU LOOSEN STRAPS "A", REMOVE BACKPACK CONTENTS (IN SEPARATE BAGS), AND UNZIP INTERNAL DIVIDER "B" YOU ARE READY TO JUMP IN AND GO TO SLEEP. THE INNER SURFACE OF THE PACK IS INSULATED WITH A REFLECTIVE MATERIAL WHICH KEEPS BODY HEAT INSIDE. A CUSHIONED MINI-SEAT IS PROVIDED, TOO.

DIVIDER "B"

STRAPS "A"

EMERGENCY RATIONS

TENTS

THE BOULDER

THE TENT!

THE *BOULDER* IS A TENT DESIGN WHICH SERIOUSLY ADDRESSES THE PROBLEM OF MOUNTAIN VANDALISM. PITCH THIS TENT AND IT MELTS INTO THE SURROUNDINGS. NO ONE WILL KNOW YOU'RE THERE!

TENT POLE SECTION PIECES

SAMPLE TENT POLE CONFIGURATION

SPECIFY BOULDER PATTERN AND COLOR (CHERT, GRANITE, SANDSTONE, ETC.)

THE WATERWALL

THE *WATERWALL* IS DESIGNED TO ACCEPT A SERIES OF CONNECTED PLASTIC SOLAR HEATING TANKS. WATER IS SIPHONED FROM AN UPHILL WATER SOURCE. TENT IS SITED TO GET SOUTHERN EXPOSURE. HEATING TANKS ARE EASILY DRAINED AND ARE COLLAPSIBLE.

SIPHON FOOTPUMP

INSULATED, REFLECTIVE TENT FLAPS ARE OPENED ON SUNNY MORNINGS, CLOSED IN INCLEMENT WEATHER AND IN THE LATE AFTERNOON.

THE ROWTENT

FOR THE FIRST TIME IN HISTORY IT IS NOW SAFE TO CAMP IN DRY CREEK-BEDS. FLASH FLOODS ARE NO PROBLEM FOR THE OCCUPANTS OF THE *ROWTENT*. ANOTHER UNIQUE ADVANTAGE OF THE *ROWTENT* IS THAT YOU CAN PITCH THE TENT IN A LAKE AND FLOAT AROUND AT NIGHT.

THE JOYS OF MOTORBOATING ARE AVAILABLE TO *ROWTENT* OWNERS.

UMBRELLA TENT

THE EASIEST TENT IN THE WORLD TO SET UP. WORKS LIKE AN ORDINARY UMBRELLA.

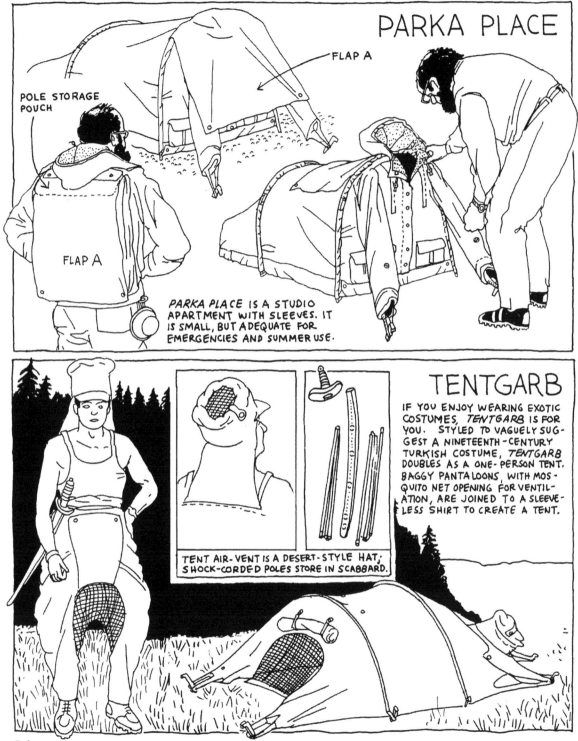

PARKA PLACE

FLAP A

POLE STORAGE POUCH

FLAP A

PARKA PLACE IS A STUDIO APARTMENT WITH SLEEVES. IT IS SMALL, BUT ADEQUATE FOR EMERGENCIES AND SUMMER USE.

TENTGARB

IF YOU ENJOY WEARING EXOTIC COSTUMES, *TENTGARB* IS FOR YOU. STYLED TO VAGUELY SUGGEST A NINETEENTH-CENTURY TURKISH COSTUME, *TENTGARB* DOUBLES AS A ONE-PERSON TENT. BAGGY PANTALOONS, WITH MOSQUITO NET OPENING FOR VENTILATION, ARE JOINED TO A SLEEVELESS SHIRT TO CREATE A TENT.

TENT AIR-VENT IS A DESERT-STYLE HAT; SHOCK-CORDED POLES STORE IN SCABBARD.

BUNKTENT

THE *BUNKTENT* EXPERIENCE IS A FAVORABLE ONE FOR YOUNG FAMILIES WHOSE CHILDREN ARE UNACCUSTOMED TO SLEEPING ALONE IN THE OUTDOORS. TWO-STORY TENTING IS AN ECONOMICAL USE OF SPACE IN CROWDED CAMPSITES.

SIERRA SAUNA

SIERRA SAUNA

COLD AIR INTAKE

DRY SAUNA

TEA KETTLE

FOR A STEAM BATH, CONNECT TUBING TO THE SPECIAL TEA KETTLE. ALL CLOTHING ITEMS, AND SLEEPING BAG SHOULD BE PLACED OUTSIDE TENT.

FOR A DRY HEAT SAUNA, PLACE THE FIRE PIT TUBING IN THE MIDST OF A CAMPFIRE AND CONNECT TUBING TO THE *SIERRA SAUNA*. A HOT BED OF COALS WILL KEEP THE TENT REASONABLY WARM FOR HOURS.

CAMPING AND SURVIVAL GEAR 95

PACK TENT

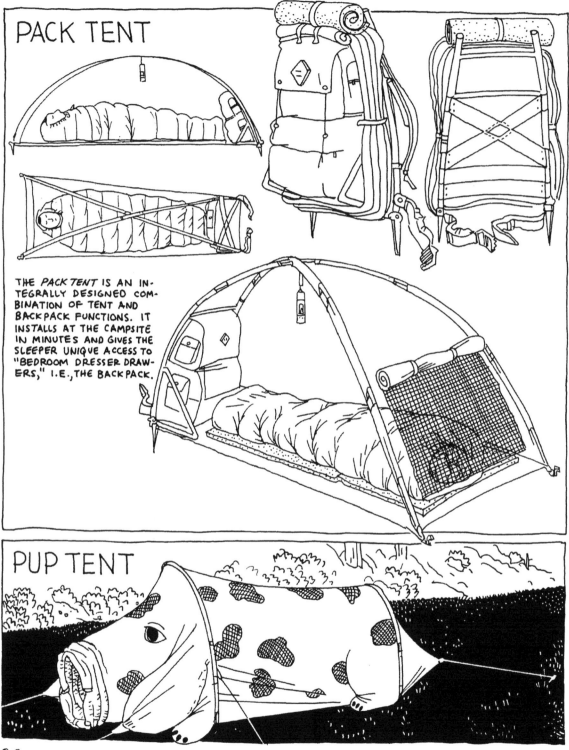

THE *PACK TENT* IS AN INTEGRALLY DESIGNED COMBINATION OF TENT AND BACKPACK FUNCTIONS. IT INSTALLS AT THE CAMPSITE IN MINUTES AND GIVES THE SLEEPER UNIQUE ACCESS TO "BEDROOM DRESSER DRAWERS," I.E., THE BACKPACK.

PUP TENT

THE FOUR-SEASON INSOMNIAC

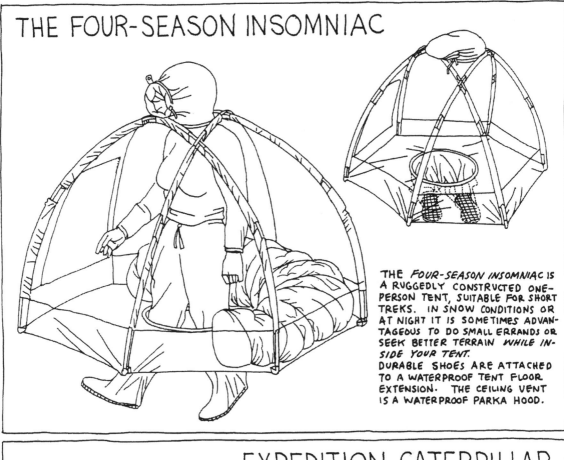

THE *FOUR-SEASON INSOMNIAC* IS A RUGGEDLY CONSTRUCTED ONE-PERSON TENT, SUITABLE FOR SHORT TREKS. IN SNOW CONDITIONS OR AT NIGHT IT IS SOMETIMES ADVANTAGEOUS TO DO SMALL ERRANDS OR SEEK BETTER TERRAIN *WHILE INSIDE YOUR TENT*.
DURABLE SHOES ARE ATTACHED TO A WATERPROOF TENT FLOOR EXTENSION. THE CEILING VENT IS A WATERPROOF PARKA HOOD.

EXPEDITION CATERPILLAR

THREE OR FOUR MOUNTAINEERS SNUGGLE COMFORTABLY IN THE *EXPEDITION CATERPILLAR*. ITS BRILLIANTLY CONTRASTING YELLOW AND BLACK PATTERN GIVES IT *EXCELLENT* VISIBILITY IN CASE THE GROUP IS THE OBJECT OF A SEARCH PARTY.

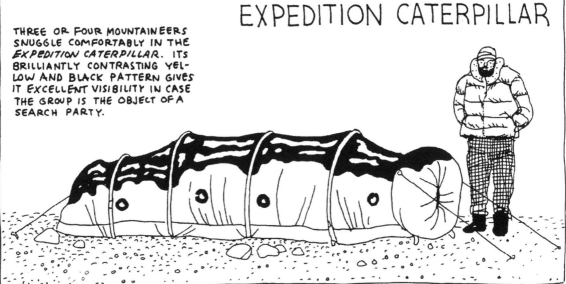

SLEEPING BAGS

MIDNIGHT MUMMY A MUMMY BAG WITH HANDS AND FEET

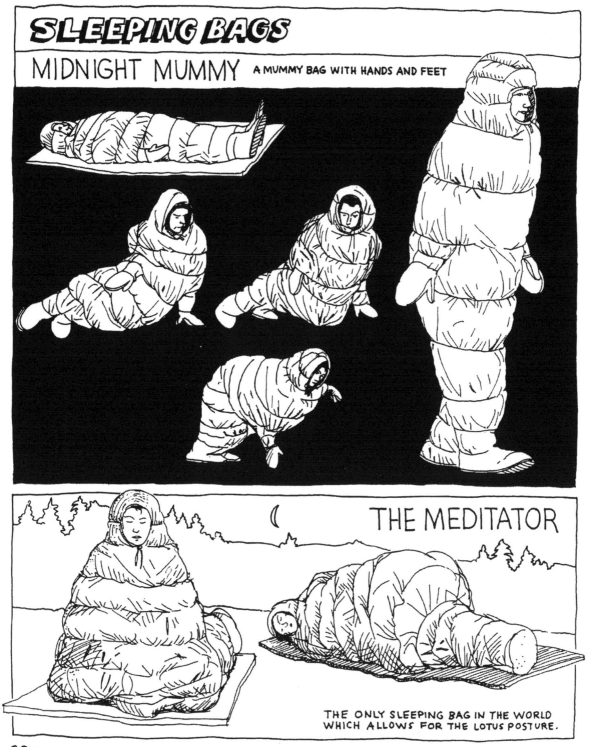

THE MEDITATOR

THE ONLY SLEEPING BAG IN THE WORLD WHICH ALLOWS FOR THE LOTUS POSTURE.

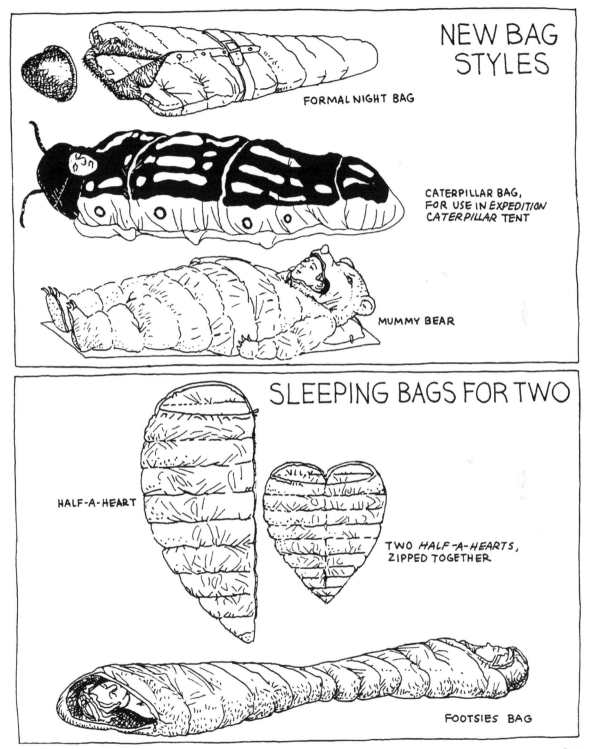

NEW BAG STYLES

FORMAL NIGHT BAG

CATERPILLAR BAG, FOR USE IN *EXPEDITION CATERPILLAR* TENT

MUMMY BEAR

SLEEPING BAGS FOR TWO

HALF-A-HEART

TWO *HALF-A-HEARTS*, ZIPPED TOGETHER

FOOTSIES BAG

SLEEPING PARKA

NOW IT IS NO LONGER NECESSARY TO CARRY BOTH A DOWN PARKA AND A SLEEPING BAG INTO THE BACKWOODS. COMPROMISES HAVE BEEN ENGINEERED TO PRODUCE A COMPOSITE DESIGN. SLEEVES (NOT SHOWN) MAY BE ATTACHED IF EXTREME WEATHER IS ANTICIPATED.

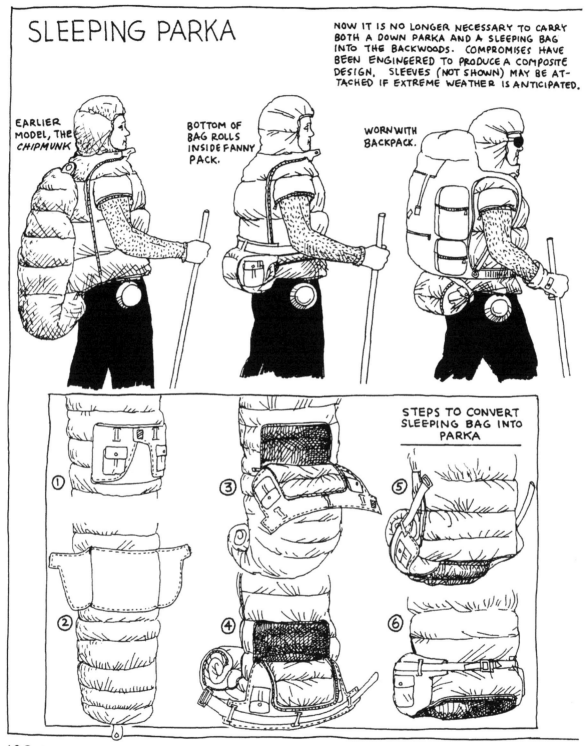

EARLIER MODEL, THE *CHIPMUNK*

BOTTOM OF BAG ROLLS INSIDE FANNY PACK.

WORN WITH BACKPACK.

STEPS TO CONVERT SLEEPING BAG INTO PARKA

① ② ③ ④ ⑤ ⑥

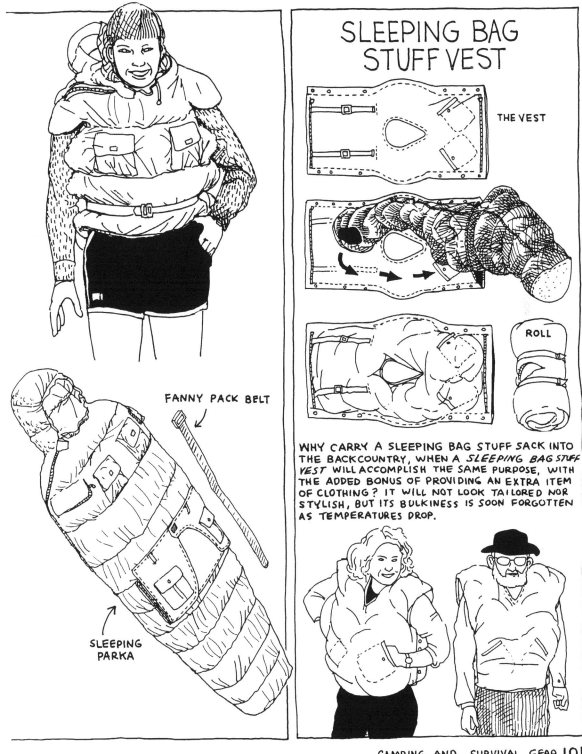

SLEEPING BAG STUFF VEST

THE VEST

ROLL

WHY CARRY A SLEEPING BAG STUFF SACK INTO THE BACKCOUNTRY, WHEN A *SLEEPING BAG STUFF VEST* WILL ACCOMPLISH THE SAME PURPOSE, WITH THE ADDED BONUS OF PROVIDING AN EXTRA ITEM OF CLOTHING? IT WILL NOT LOOK TAILORED NOR STYLISH, BUT ITS BULKINESS IS SOON FORGOTTEN AS TEMPERATURES DROP.

FANNY PACK BELT

SLEEPING PARKA

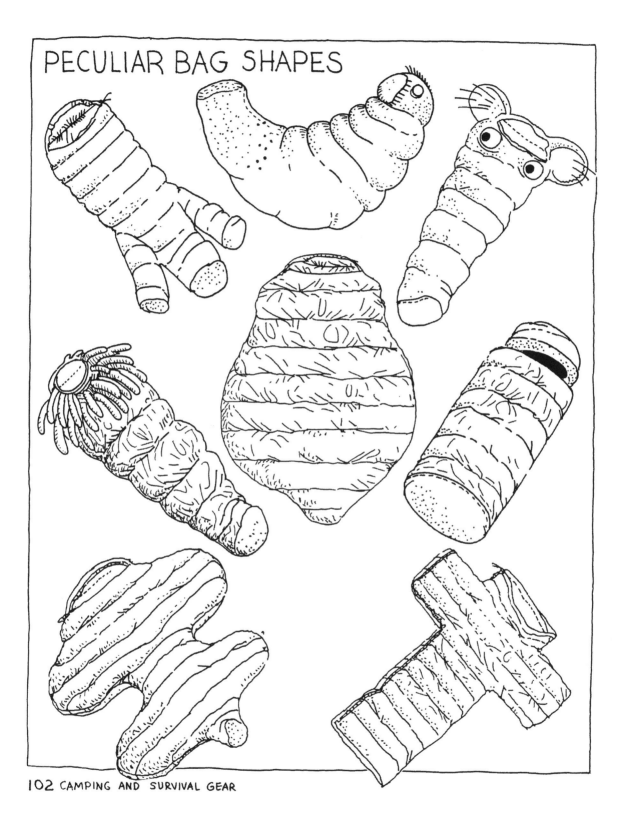

PECULIAR BAG SHAPES

AQUATIC AND REPTILIAN BAG STYLES

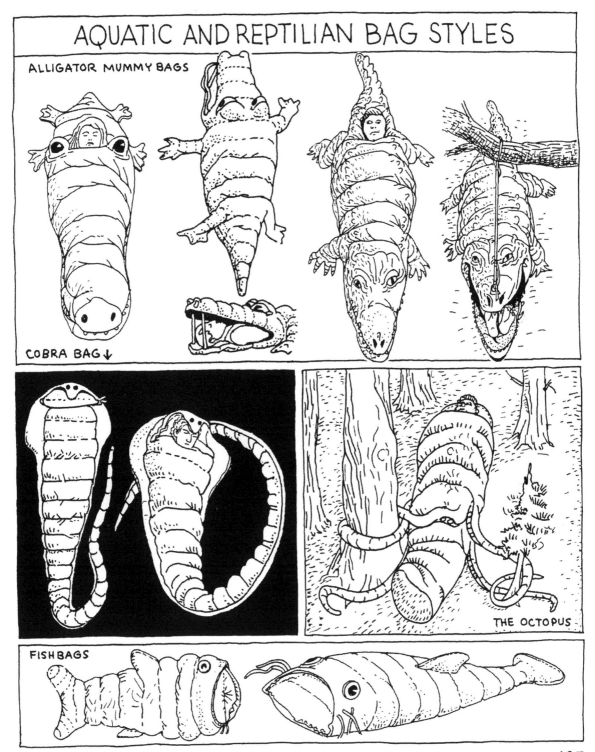

ALLIGATOR MUMMY BAGS

COBRA BAG ↓

THE OCTOPUS

FISHBAGS

HUNTING SUITS

LOGBLIND

GAMESUIT

WINE

BOTA BALACLAVA

LOGBLIND IS A WATER-PROOF CONCEALMENT UNIT WITH COMFORTABLE PLEATED SKIRT FOR EASY WALKING. BREATHABLE FABRIC WITH BOGUS FOLIAGE. TWO-WAY COMMUNICATION RADIO.

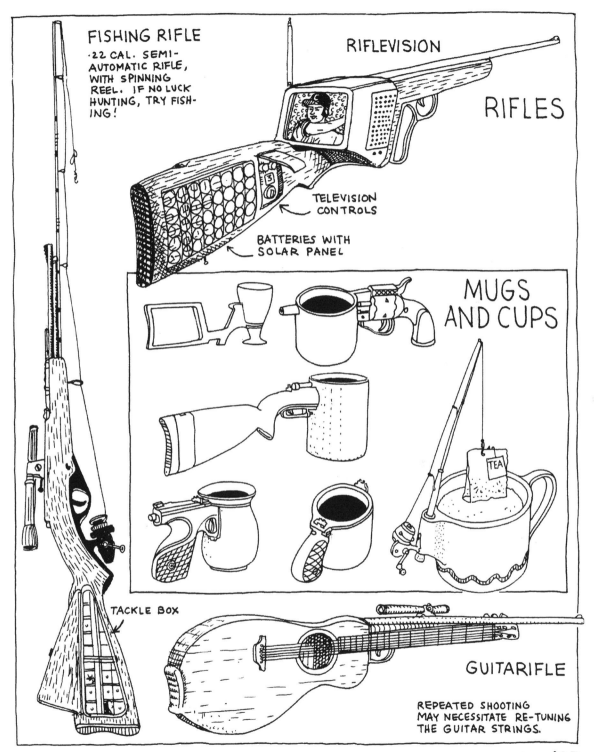

FISHING RIFLE

.22 CAL. SEMI-
AUTOMATIC RIFLE,
WITH SPINNING
REEL. IF NO LUCK
HUNTING, TRY FISH-
ING!

RIFLEVISION

RIFLES

TELEVISION
CONTROLS

BATTERIES WITH
SOLAR PANEL

MUGS
AND CUPS

TEA

TACKLE BOX

GUITARIFLE

REPEATED SHOOTING
MAY NECESSITATE RE-TUNING
THE GUITAR STRINGS.

350 CC TRAILBUCK

ALSO NICKNAMED
"ENTRAIL BIKE"

HARD RUBBER
FAKE ANTLERS

SLINGSHOT HUNTING SHOES

AMMO

THE THICKET
FOUR-WHEEL DRIVE

CAMOUFLAGE-WALL
TIRES!

SHOOTING GLASSES

GLASSES WITH EARPLUGS

LOOSEN TO ADJUST LENGTH, AND INSERT IN EARS.

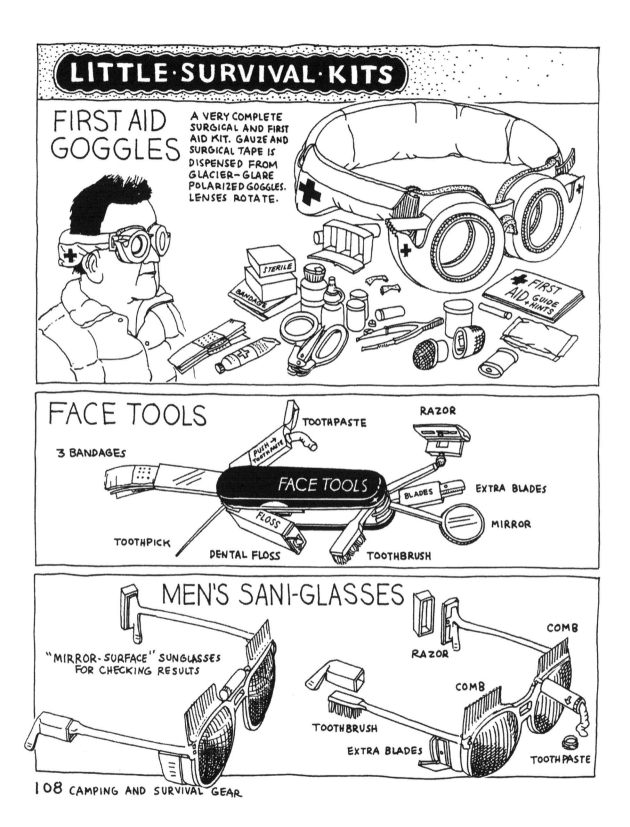

LITTLE·SURVIVAL·KITS

FIRST AID GOGGLES

A VERY COMPLETE SURGICAL AND FIRST AID KIT. GAUZE AND SURGICAL TAPE IS DISPENSED FROM GLACIER-GLARE POLARIZED GOGGLES. LENSES ROTATE.

STERILE

BANDAGE

FIRST AID GUIDE + HINTS

FACE TOOLS

3 BANDAGES

TOOTHPASTE

PUSH → TOOTHPASTE

RAZOR

FACE TOOLS

BLADES

EXTRA BLADES

MIRROR

TOOTHPICK

FLOSS

DENTAL FLOSS

TOOTHBRUSH

MEN'S SANI-GLASSES

"MIRROR-SURFACE" SUNGLASSES FOR CHECKING RESULTS

RAZOR

COMB

COMB

TOOTHBRUSH

EXTRA BLADES

TOOTHPASTE

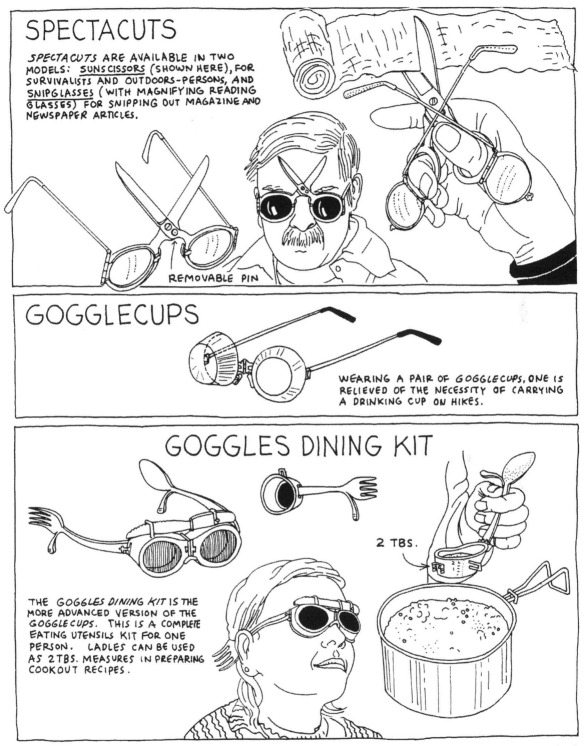

SPECTACUTS

SPECTACUTS ARE AVAILABLE IN TWO MODELS: <u>SUNSCISSORS</u> (SHOWN HERE), FOR SURVIVALISTS AND OUTDOORS-PERSONS, AND <u>SNIPGLASSES</u> (WITH MAGNIFYING READING GLASSES) FOR SNIPPING OUT MAGAZINE AND NEWSPAPER ARTICLES.

REMOVABLE PIN

GOGGLECUPS

WEARING A PAIR OF *GOGGLECUPS*, ONE IS RELIEVED OF THE NECESSITY OF CARRYING A DRINKING CUP ON HIKES.

GOGGLES DINING KIT

2 TBS.

THE *GOGGLES DINING KIT* IS THE MORE ADVANCED VERSION OF THE *GOGGLECUPS*. THIS IS A COMPLETE EATING UTENSILS KIT FOR ONE PERSON. LADLES CAN BE USED AS 2 TBS. MEASURES IN PREPARING COOKOUT RECIPES.

CAMP COOK KITS

UKULELE COOK KIT

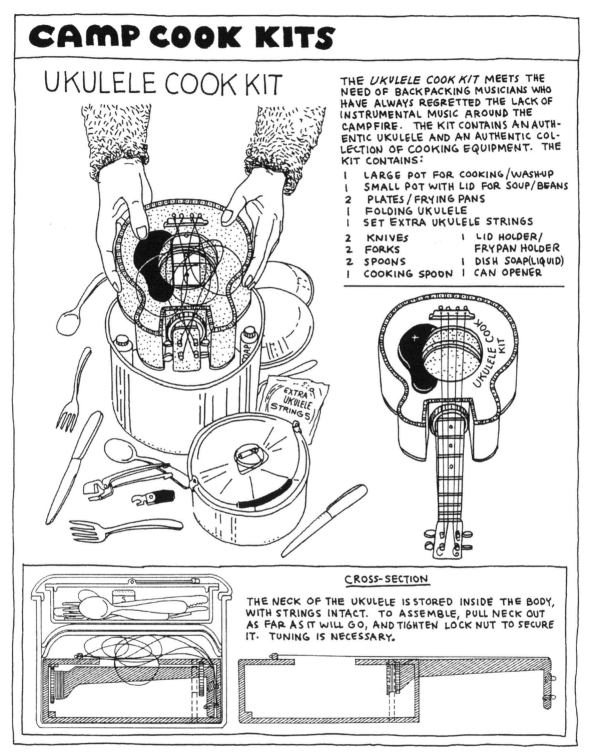

THE *UKULELE COOK KIT* MEETS THE
NEED OF BACKPACKING MUSICIANS WHO
HAVE ALWAYS REGRETTED THE LACK OF
INSTRUMENTAL MUSIC AROUND THE
CAMPFIRE. THE KIT CONTAINS AN AUTH-
ENTIC UKULELE AND AN AUTHENTIC COL-
LECTION OF COOKING EQUIPMENT. THE
KIT CONTAINS:

1 LARGE POT FOR COOKING/WASH-UP
1 SMALL POT WITH LID FOR SOUP/BEANS
2 PLATES / FRYING PANS
1 FOLDING UKULELE
1 SET EXTRA UKULELE STRINGS

2 KNIVES	1 LID HOLDER/
2 FORKS	FRYPAN HOLDER
2 SPOONS	1 DISH SOAP(LIQUID)
1 COOKING SPOON	1 CAN OPENER

EXTRA
UKULELE
STRINGS

UKULELE COOK KIT

CROSS-SECTION

THE NECK OF THE UKULELE IS STORED INSIDE THE BODY,
WITH STRINGS INTACT. TO ASSEMBLE, PULL NECK OUT
AS FAR AS IT WILL GO, AND TIGHTEN LOCK NUT TO SECURE
IT. TUNING IS NECESSARY.

MESS KIT UMBRELLA

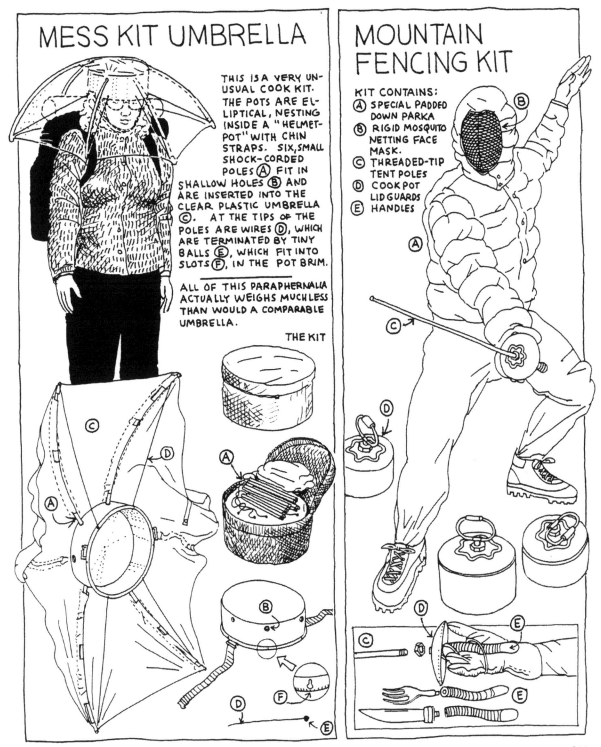

THIS IS A VERY UN-USUAL COOK KIT. THE POTS ARE EL-LIPTICAL, NESTING INSIDE A "HELMET-POT" WITH CHIN STRAPS. SIX, SMALL SHOCK-CORDED POLES Ⓐ FIT IN SHALLOW HOLES Ⓑ AND ARE INSERTED INTO THE CLEAR PLASTIC UMBRELLA Ⓒ. AT THE TIPS OF THE POLES ARE WIRES Ⓓ, WHICH ARE TERMINATED BY TINY BALLS Ⓔ, WHICH FIT INTO SLOTS Ⓕ, IN THE POT BRIM.

ALL OF THIS PARAPHERNALIA ACTUALLY WEIGHS MUCH LESS THAN WOULD A COMPARABLE UMBRELLA.

THE KIT

MOUNTAIN FENCING KIT

KIT CONTAINS:
Ⓐ SPECIAL PADDED DOWN PARKA
Ⓑ RIGID MOSQUITO NETTING FACE MASK.
Ⓒ THREADED-TIP TENT POLES
Ⓓ COOK POT LID GUARDS
Ⓔ HANDLES

ARMPUMPS
SWEATSHIRT

AIR-PAULETS

RECREATIONAL PUMPWEAR

CLOTHING ITEMS FOR
INFLATING VOLLEYBALLS,
AIR MATTRESSES, ETC. AND
FANNING CAMPFIRE.

PUMP HAT AND
PUMPSHOES

SNAKEBOOTS

HIKING IN SNAKE COUNTRY CAN BE UNNERVING, BUT IF YOU ARE WEARING THE *SNAKEBOOTS*, YOU WILL HAVE A SENSE OF SECURITY.

BOGBOOTS

THE STYLING OF *BOGBOOTS* MIMICS THE WIDE STANCE OF AQUATIC AND SHORELINE BIRDS, AMPHIBIANS, AND REPTILES.

BACKPACKERS' INVERSION BOOT KIT

THROW ROPE OVER TREE, PULL YOURSELF UP.

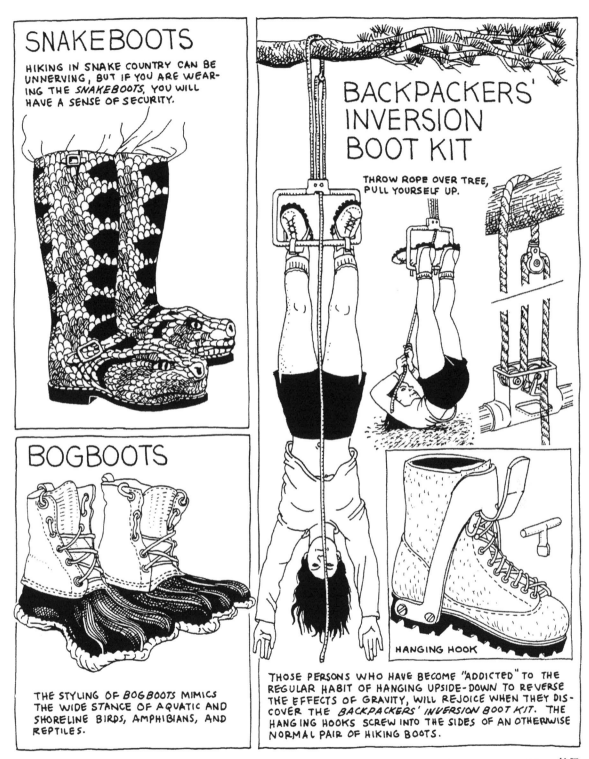

HANGING HOOK

THOSE PERSONS WHO HAVE BECOME "ADDICTED" TO THE REGULAR HABIT OF HANGING UPSIDE-DOWN TO REVERSE THE EFFECTS OF GRAVITY, WILL REJOICE WHEN THEY DISCOVER THE *BACKPACKERS' INVERSION BOOT KIT*. THE HANGING HOOKS SCREW INTO THE SIDES OF AN OTHERWISE NORMAL PAIR OF HIKING BOOTS.

COLD WEATHER HEADGEAR

3-WAY HAT

SUNNY

CHILLY

STORMY

DUCKBILL

TANHAT

REFLECTIVE SURFACE FOR TANNING, FOLD BACK IF TOO MUCH GLARE

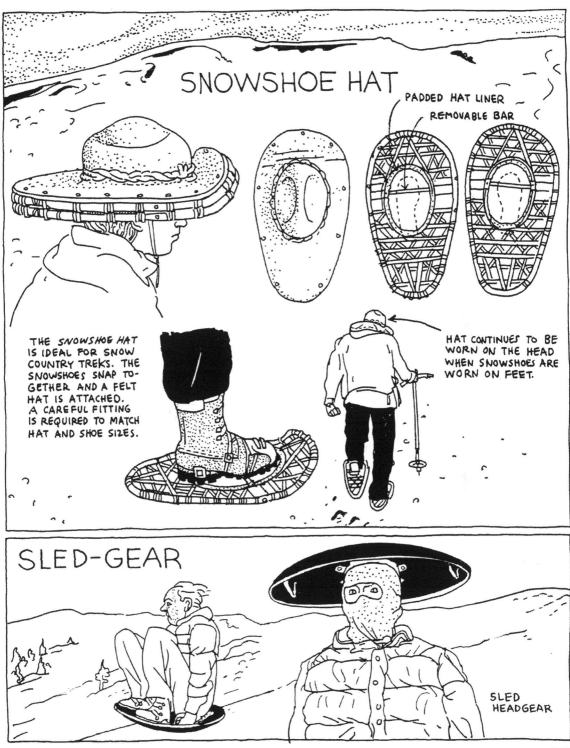

SNOWSHOE HAT

PADDED HAT LINER

REMOVABLE BAR

THE *SNOWSHOE HAT* IS IDEAL FOR SNOW COUNTRY TREKS. THE SNOWSHOES SNAP TOGETHER AND A FELT HAT IS ATTACHED. A CAREFUL FITTING IS REQUIRED TO MATCH HAT AND SHOE SIZES.

HAT CONTINUES TO BE WORN ON THE HEAD WHEN SNOWSHOES ARE WORN ON FEET.

SLED-GEAR

SLED HEADGEAR

ELEPHANT MAN PARKA

IN EXTREMELY COLD WEATHER, THE EARS MAY BE SNAPPED TOGETHER IN FRONT OF THE FACE. THE AIR-INTAKE (TRUNK) IS WARMED BY PLACING IT UNDER THE ARMPIT.

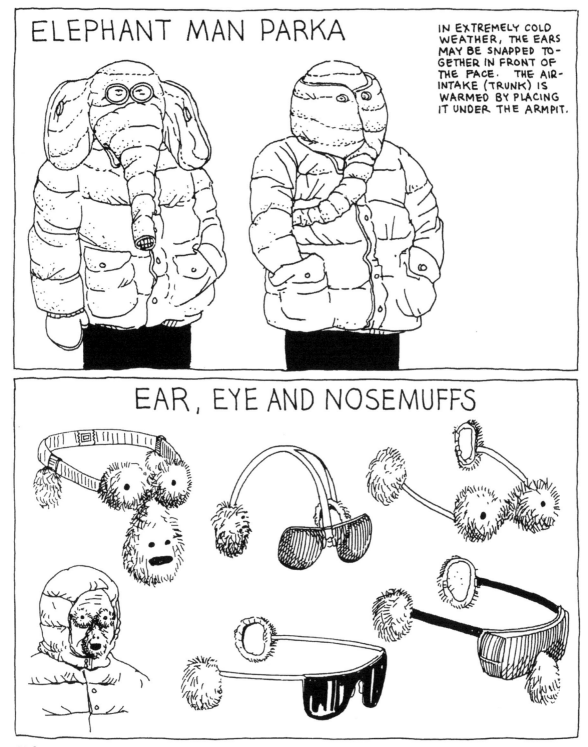

EAR, EYE AND NOSEMUFFS

TRANSPORTATION

BICYCLES

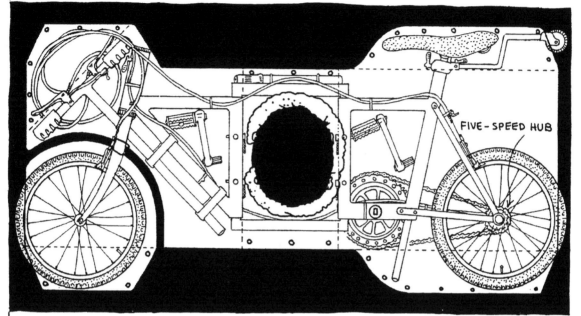

FIVE-SPEED HUB

THE BIKE VEST

MANY "SURVIVALISTS" ENVISION A DAY IN THE FUTURE WHEN URBAN DWELLERS WILL BE SCRAMBLING TO GET TO THE WOODS, THE HILLS OR THE COUNTRYSIDE.

BY ADOPTING *THE BIKEVEST* AS AN ITEM OF DAILY APPAREL, ONE WILL ALWAYS BE READY! WHILE AUTOS ARE AT A STANDSTILL ON CLOGGED FREEWAYS, THE *BIKEVEST* GOES AHEAD.

SOME PERSONS MAY PREFER TO WEAR *THE BIKEVEST* LESS OBTRUSIVELY, BY DONNING THE FITTED PARKA SHELL.

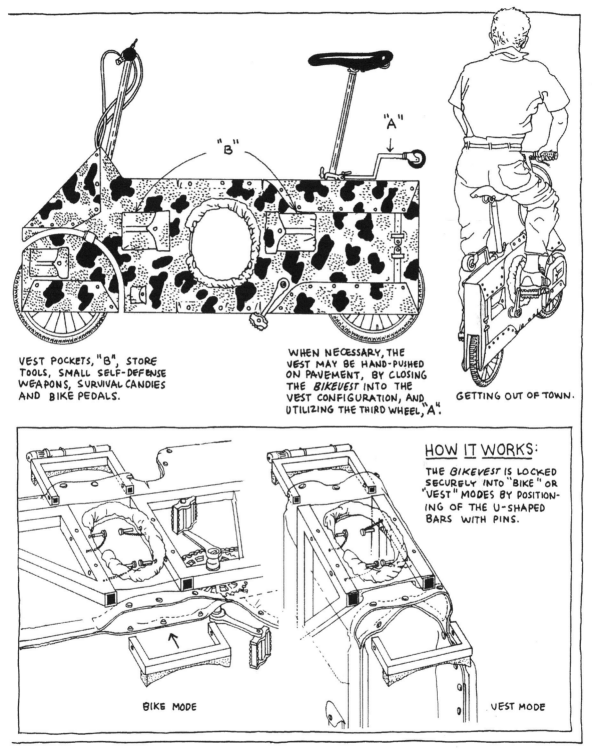

VEST POCKETS, "B", STORE
TOOLS, SMALL SELF-DEFENSE
WEAPONS, SURVIVAL CANDIES
AND BIKE PEDALS.

WHEN NECESSARY, THE
VEST MAY BE HAND-PUSHED
ON PAVEMENT, BY CLOSING
THE BIKEVEST INTO THE
VEST CONFIGURATION, AND
UTILIZING THE THIRD WHEEL, "A".

GETTING OUT OF TOWN.

HOW IT WORKS:

THE BIKEVEST IS LOCKED
SECURELY INTO "BIKE" OR
"VEST" MODES BY POSITION-
ING OF THE U-SHAPED
BARS WITH PINS.

BIKE MODE

VEST MODE

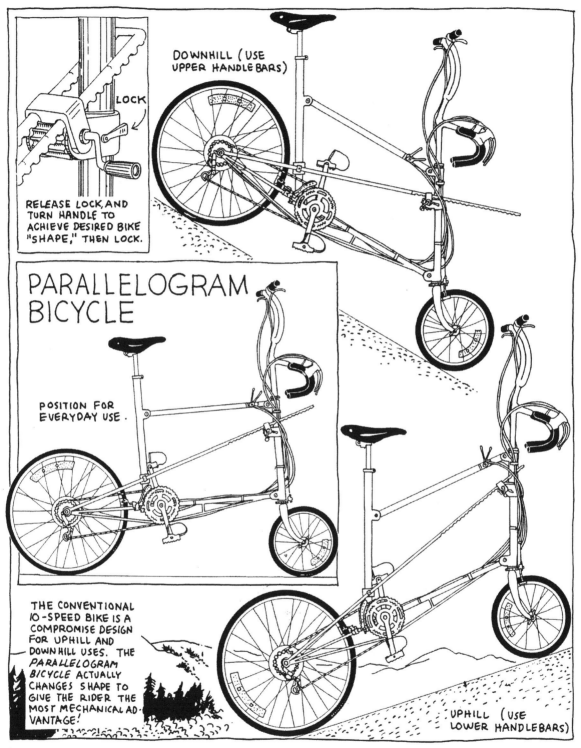

RELEASE LOCK, AND TURN HANDLE TO ACHIEVE DESIRED BIKE "SHAPE," THEN LOCK.

LOCK

DOWNHILL (USE UPPER HANDLEBARS)

PARALLELOGRAM BICYCLE

POSITION FOR EVERYDAY USE.

THE CONVENTIONAL 10-SPEED BIKE IS A COMPROMISE DESIGN FOR UPHILL AND DOWNHILL USES. THE *PARALLELOGRAM BICYCLE* ACTUALLY CHANGES SHAPE TO GIVE THE RIDER THE MOST MECHANICAL ADVANTAGE!

UPHILL (USE LOWER HANDLEBARS)

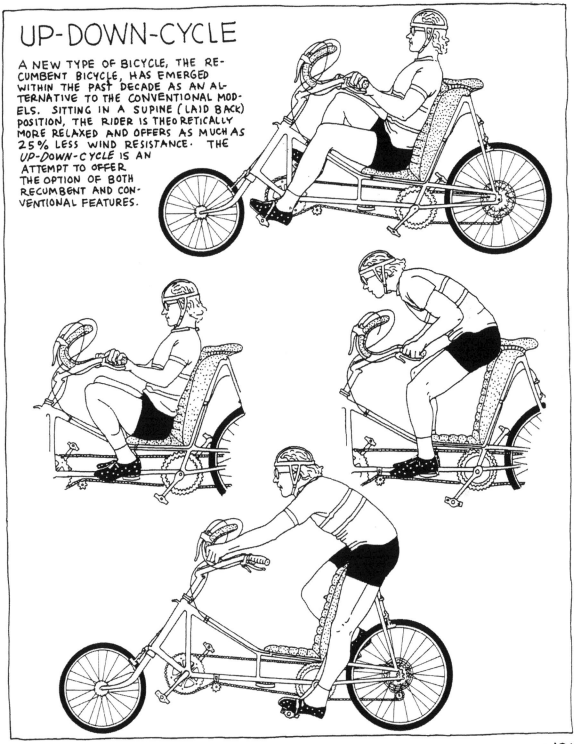

UP-DOWN-CYCLE

A NEW TYPE OF BICYCLE, THE RE-CUMBENT BICYCLE, HAS EMERGED WITHIN THE PAST DECADE AS AN AL-TERNATIVE TO THE CONVENTIONAL MOD-ELS. SITTING IN A SUPINE (LAID BACK) POSITION, THE RIDER IS THEORETICALLY MORE RELAXED AND OFFERS AS MUCH AS 25% LESS WIND RESISTANCE. THE *UP-DOWN-CYCLE* IS AN ATTEMPT TO OFFER THE OPTION OF BOTH RECUMBENT AND CON-VENTIONAL FEATURES.

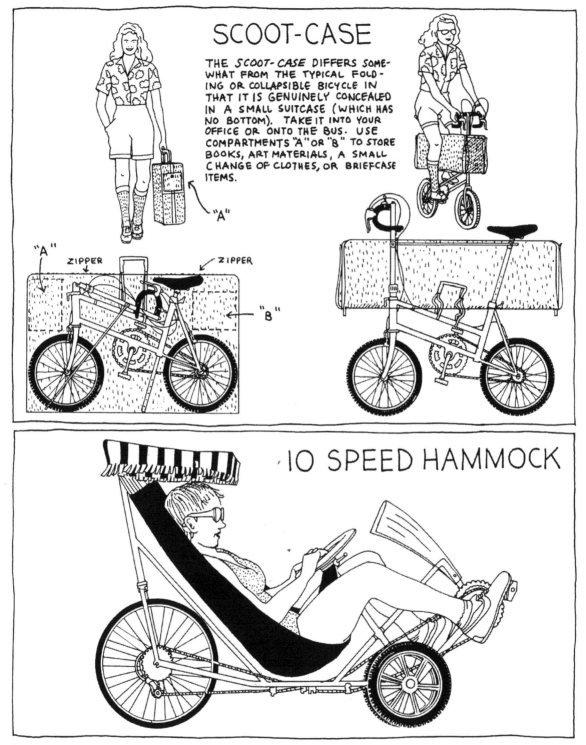

SCOOT-CASE

THE *SCOOT-CASE* DIFFERS SOME-
WHAT FROM THE TYPICAL FOLD-
ING OR COLLAPSIBLE BICYCLE IN
THAT IT IS GENUINELY CONCEALED
IN A SMALL SUITCASE (WHICH HAS
NO BOTTOM). TAKE IT INTO YOUR
OFFICE OR ONTO THE BUS. USE
COMPARTMENTS "A" OR "B" TO STORE
BOOKS, ART MATERIALS, A SMALL
CHANGE OF CLOTHES, OR BRIEFCASE
ITEMS.

"A"

"A"

ZIPPER

ZIPPER

"B"

IO SPEED HAMMOCK

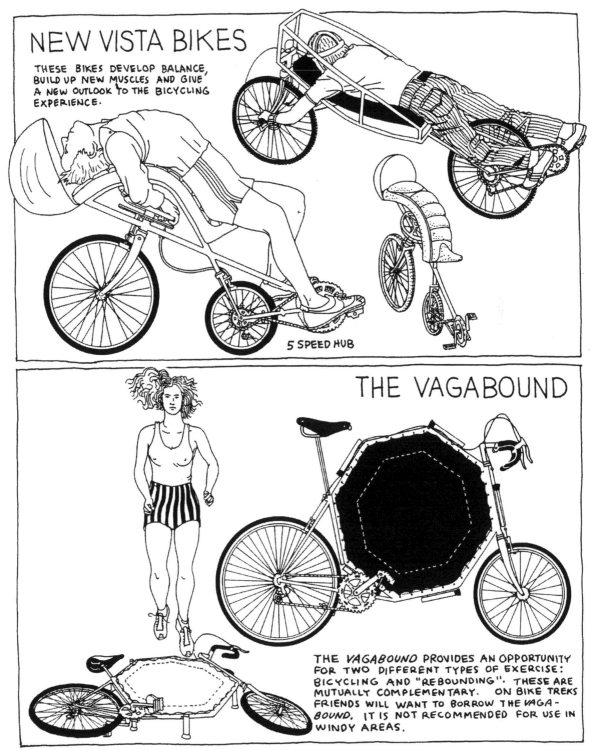

NEW VISTA BIKES

THESE BIKES DEVELOP BALANCE, BUILD UP NEW MUSCLES AND GIVE A NEW OUTLOOK TO THE BICYCLING EXPERIENCE.

5 SPEED HUB

THE VAGABOUND

THE *VAGABOUND* PROVIDES AN OPPORTUNITY FOR TWO DIFFERENT TYPES OF EXERCISE: BICYCLING AND "REBOUNDING". THESE ARE MUTUALLY COMPLEMENTARY. ON BIKE TREKS FRIENDS WILL WANT TO BORROW THE *VAGA-BOUND*. IT IS NOT RECOMMENDED FOR USE IN WINDY AREAS.

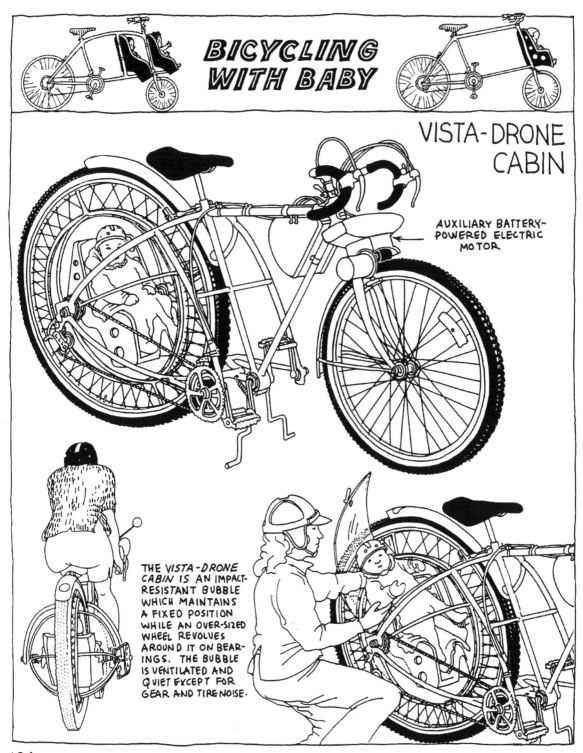

BICYCLING WITH BABY

VISTA-DRONE CABIN

AUXILIARY BATTERY-POWERED ELECTRIC MOTOR

THE VISTA-DRONE CABIN IS AN IMPACT-RESISTANT BUBBLE WHICH MAINTAINS A FIXED POSITION WHILE AN OVER-SIZED WHEEL REVOLVES AROUND IT ON BEARINGS. THE BUBBLE IS VENTILATED AND QUIET EXCEPT FOR GEAR AND TIRE NOISE.

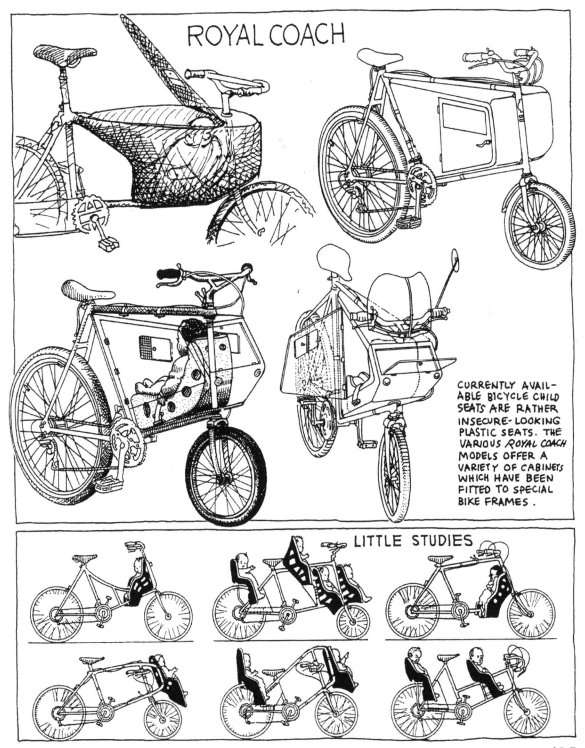

ROYAL COACH

CURRENTLY AVAILABLE BICYCLE CHILD SEATS ARE RATHER INSECURE-LOOKING PLASTIC SEATS. THE VARIOUS *ROYAL COACH* MODELS OFFER A VARIETY OF CABINETS WHICH HAVE BEEN FITTED TO SPECIAL BIKE FRAMES.

LITTLE STUDIES

BICYCLE FRAMES

THE PUSH TO ACHIEVE
LIGHTER AND MORE EF-
FICIENT BICYCLE FRAMES
HAS HAD REMARKABLE
RESULTS, BUT WHIMSY,
ORNAMENTATION, AND
ARTISTIC EXPRESSION
HAVE BEEN PUSHED
ASIDE. WITH LIGHTER
ALLOYS FROM THE SPACE
AND AIRCRAFT INDUSTRIES,
IT WOULD BE FUN TO
GET SILLY WITH BIKE
FRAME DESIGN.

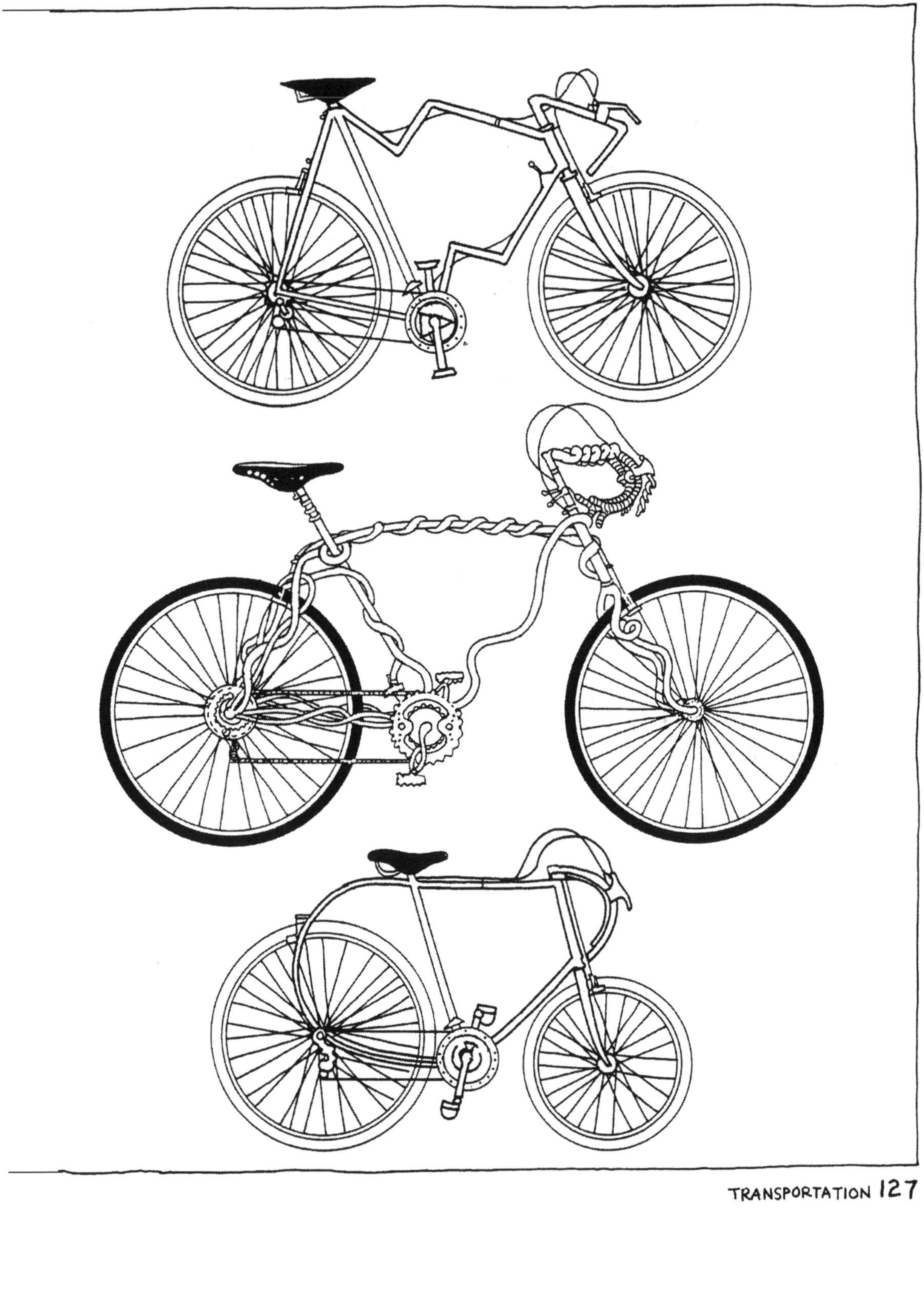

NEW ANTIQUE BIKE FRAMES

EVERY RACING BIKE AND 10-SPEED THAT PLIES THE HIGHWAYS AND SUBURBAN STREETS LOOKS DREARILY SIMILAR. IT'S TIME TO BRING PECULIARITY, IDIOSYNCRACY, AND INDIVIDUALITY INTO BIKE DESIGN.

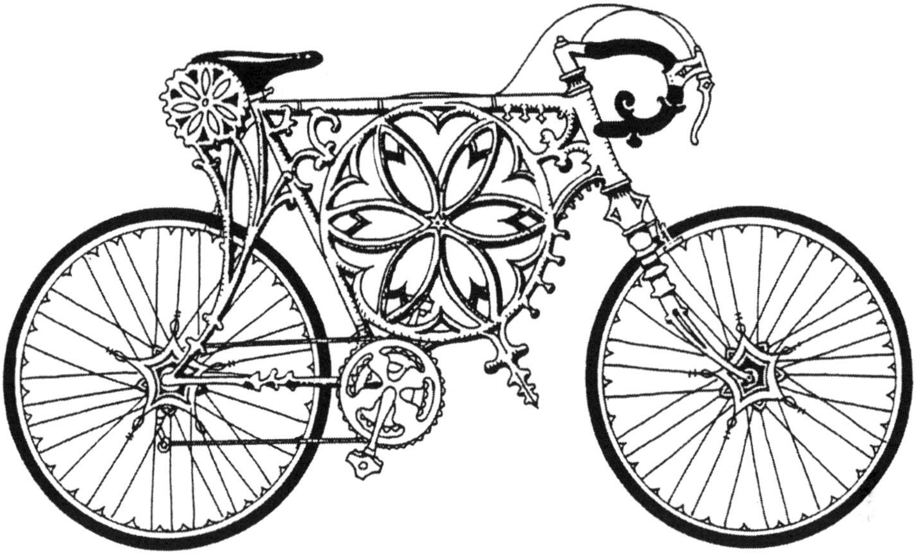

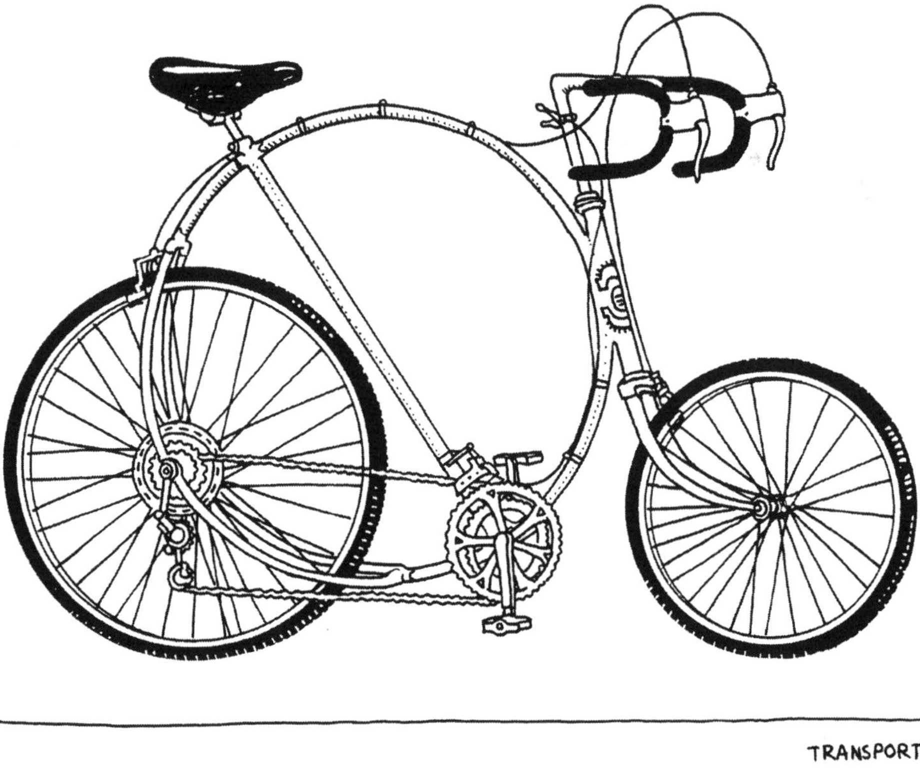

MOTORCYCLES

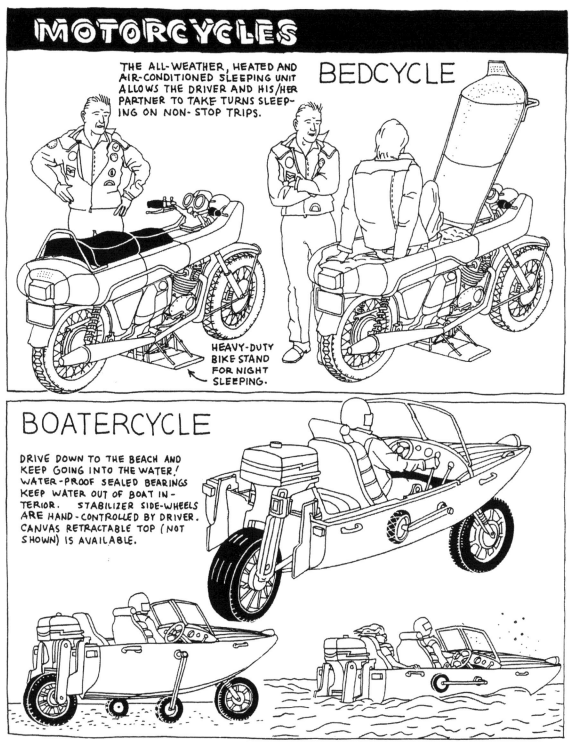

THE ALL-WEATHER, HEATED AND AIR-CONDITIONED SLEEPING UNIT ALLOWS THE DRIVER AND HIS/HER PARTNER TO TAKE TURNS SLEEPING ON NON-STOP TRIPS.

BEDCYCLE

HEAVY-DUTY BIKE STAND FOR NIGHT SLEEPING.

BOATERCYCLE

DRIVE DOWN TO THE BEACH AND KEEP GOING INTO THE WATER! WATER-PROOF SEALED BEARINGS KEEP WATER OUT OF BOAT INTERIOR. STABILIZER SIDE-WHEELS ARE HAND-CONTROLLED BY DRIVER. CANVAS RETRACTABLE TOP (NOT SHOWN) IS AVAILABLE.

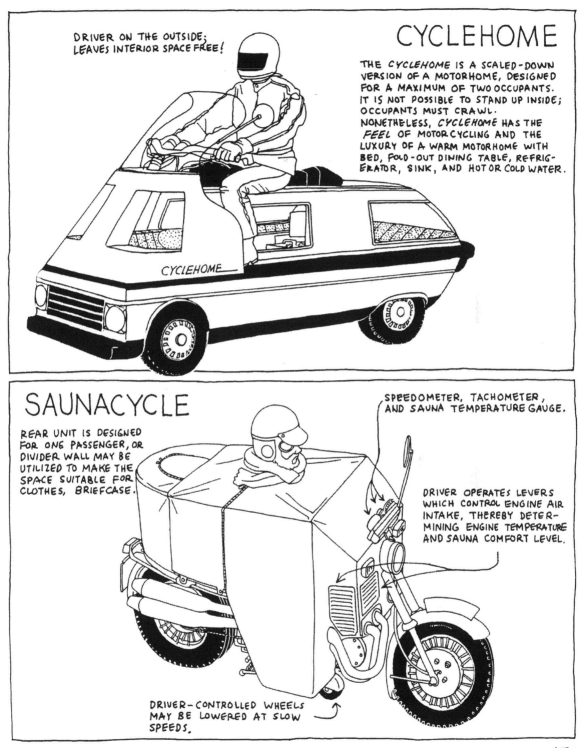

CYCLEHOME

DRIVER ON THE OUTSIDE; LEAVES INTERIOR SPACE FREE!

THE *CYCLEHOME* IS A SCALED-DOWN VERSION OF A MOTORHOME, DESIGNED FOR A MAXIMUM OF TWO OCCUPANTS. IT IS NOT POSSIBLE TO STAND UP INSIDE; OCCUPANTS MUST CRAWL. NONETHELESS, *CYCLEHOME* HAS THE *FEEL* OF MOTORCYCLING AND THE LUXURY OF A WARM MOTORHOME WITH BED, FOLD-OUT DINING TABLE, REFRIGERATOR, SINK, AND HOT OR COLD WATER.

CYCLEHOME

SAUNACYCLE

REAR UNIT IS DESIGNED FOR ONE PASSENGER, OR DIVIDER WALL MAY BE UTILIZED TO MAKE THE SPACE SUITABLE FOR CLOTHES, BRIEFCASE.

SPEEDOMETER, TACHOMETER, AND SAUNA TEMPERATURE GAUGE.

DRIVER OPERATES LEVERS WHICH CONTROL ENGINE AIR INTAKE, THEREBY DETERMINING ENGINE TEMPERATURE AND SAUNA COMFORT LEVEL.

DRIVER-CONTROLLED WHEELS MAY BE LOWERED AT SLOW SPEEDS.

MOTO-DINETTE

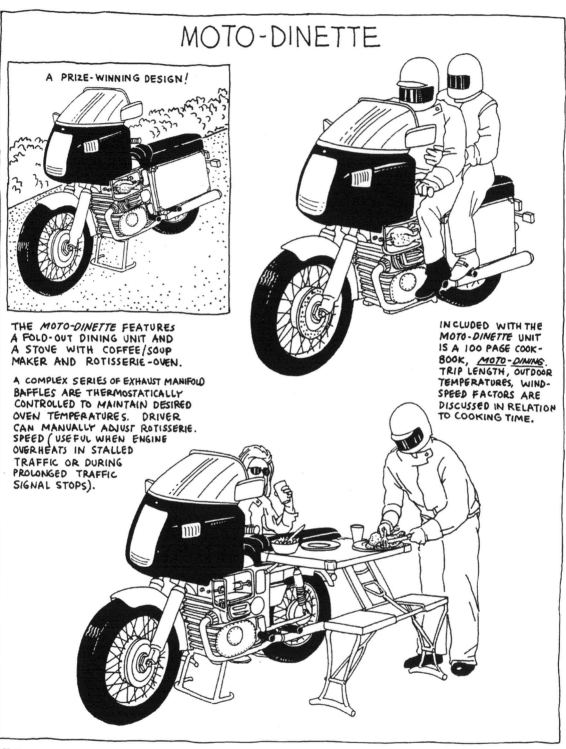

A PRIZE-WINNING DESIGN!

THE *MOTO-DINETTE* FEATURES A FOLD-OUT DINING UNIT AND A STOVE WITH COFFEE/SOUP MAKER AND ROTISSERIE-OVEN.

A COMPLEX SERIES OF EXHAUST MANIFOLD BAFFLES ARE THERMOSTATICALLY CONTROLLED TO MAINTAIN DESIRED OVEN TEMPERATURES. DRIVER CAN MANUALLY ADJUST ROTISSERIE SPEED (USEFUL WHEN ENGINE OVERHEATS IN STALLED TRAFFIC OR DURING PROLONGED TRAFFIC SIGNAL STOPS).

INCLUDED WITH THE *MOTO-DINETTE* UNIT IS A 100 PAGE COOK-BOOK, *MOTO-DINING*. TRIP LENGTH, OUTDOOR TEMPERATURES, WIND-SPEED FACTORS ARE DISCUSSED IN RELATION TO COOKING TIME.

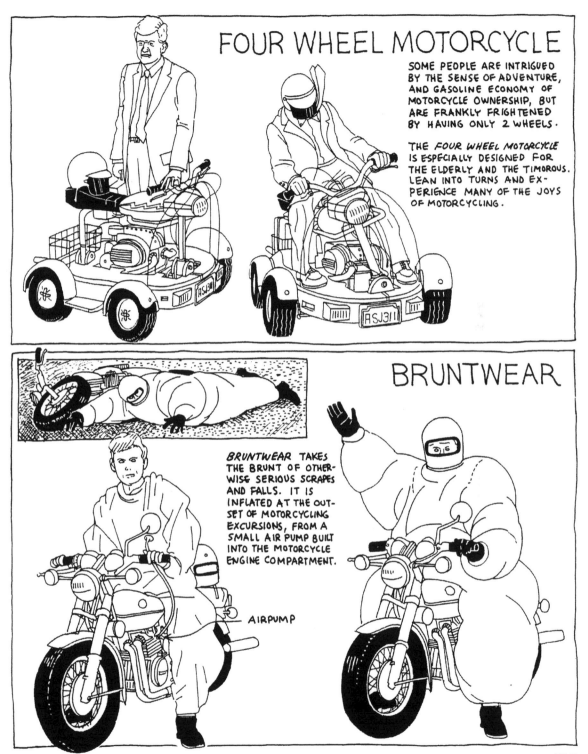

FOUR WHEEL MOTORCYCLE

SOME PEOPLE ARE INTRIGUED BY THE SENSE OF ADVENTURE, AND GASOLINE ECONOMY OF MOTORCYCLE OWNERSHIP, BUT ARE FRANKLY FRIGHTENED BY HAVING ONLY 2 WHEELS.

THE *FOUR WHEEL MOTORCYCLE* IS ESPECIALLY DESIGNED FOR THE ELDERLY AND THE TIMOROUS. LEAN INTO TURNS AND EXPERIENCE MANY OF THE JOYS OF MOTORCYCLING.

BRUNTWEAR

BRUNTWEAR TAKES THE BRUNT OF OTHERWISE SERIOUS SCRAPES AND FALLS. IT IS INFLATED AT THE OUTSET OF MOTORCYCLING EXCURSIONS, FROM A SMALL AIR PUMP BUILT INTO THE MOTORCYCLE ENGINE COMPARTMENT.

AIRPUMP

FUTURECYCLES FANTASTIC SHAPES FOR A NEW AGE

RATTANCYCLE

SMART HOMEMAKERS WHO WISH TO GIVE NEW SPARKLE TO DRAB LIVINGROOMS, WILL WANT THE *RATTANCYCLE*. INTEGRATED WITH A MATCHING ROOM GROUP, THE *RATTANCYCLE* MAY BE KEPT IN THE LIVINGROOM (WITH OIL DRIP PAN TO PROTECT CARPET).

THE DRIVER'S SEAT CAN BE MADE TO ROTATE FREELY FOR EASE OF EGRESS, IF DESIRED.

FISHCYCLE

THOSE WHO ARE DAILY SUFFERING FROM THE DEPRESSING ANONYMITY OF MODERN LIFE ARE GUARANTEED TO BE NOTICED WHEN THEY DRIVE THE *FISHCYCLE* ALONG THE FREEWAY.

TRAILBIKES

MEDIEVAL
MOTORCYCLE

60 MILES TO
THE GALLEON!

EXCEPT FOR THE LACK OF
THE NORMAL NUMBER OF
SAILS, THIS GALLEON MOTOR-
CYCLE IS AUTHENTICALLY DE-
TAILED.

AUTOMOBILES

2 WHEEL SEDAN

AUTO TRAVEL HAS GRADUALLY LOST MUCH OF ITS FORMER ADVENTUROUSNESS. THE *2 WHEEL SEDAN* IS GUARANTEED TO BRING BACK MANY OF THE FORMER THRILLS. DRIVER AND PASSENGERS *LEAN* INTO TURNS, AND THE RUSH OF ADRENALIN WILL BE FELT OFTEN. AT THE START OF A TRIP, THE DRIVER SITS IN THE MIDDLE, PASSENGERS DISTRIBUTE THEMSELVES IN SEATING ARRANGEMENTS WHICH WILL BALANCE THE WEIGHT, AND THE *LOAD-IMBALANCE COMPENSATOR* IS ADJUSTED. SIDE WHEELS RAISE AUTOMATICALLY AT SPEEDS ABOVE 5 MPH.

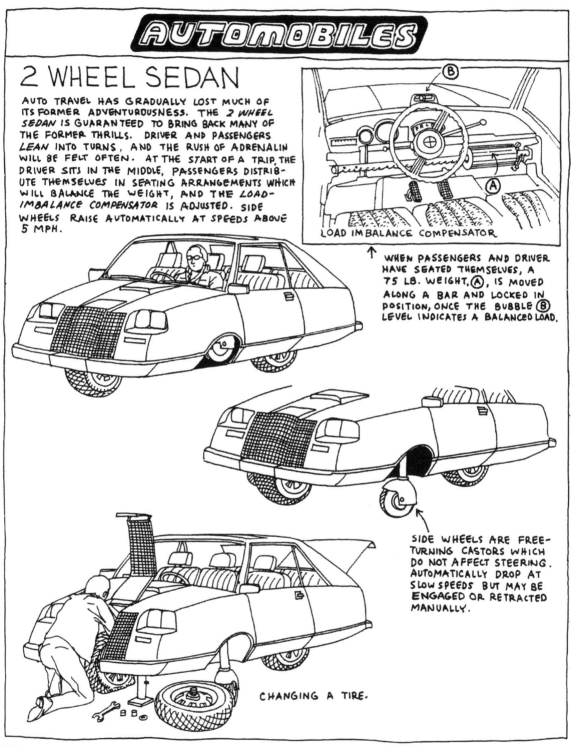

LOAD IMBALANCE COMPENSATOR

↑ WHEN PASSENGERS AND DRIVER HAVE SEATED THEMSELVES, A 75 LB. WEIGHT, Ⓐ, IS MOVED ALONG A BAR AND LOCKED IN POSITION, ONCE THE BUBBLE Ⓑ LEVEL INDICATES A BALANCED LOAD.

SIDE WHEELS ARE FREE-TURNING CASTORS WHICH DO NOT AFFECT STEERING. AUTOMATICALLY DROP AT SLOW SPEEDS BUT MAY BE ENGAGED OR RETRACTED MANUALLY.

CHANGING A TIRE.

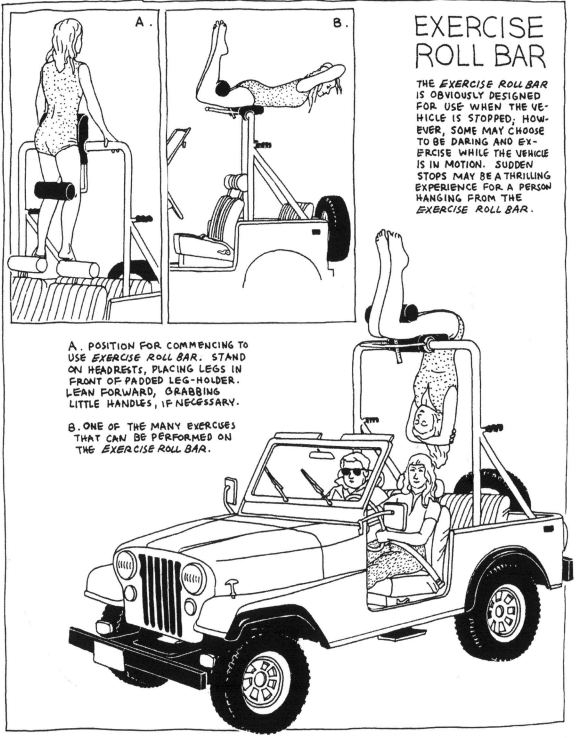

EXERCISE ROLL BAR

THE *EXERCISE ROLL BAR* IS OBVIOUSLY DESIGNED FOR USE WHEN THE VEHICLE IS STOPPED; HOWEVER, SOME MAY CHOOSE TO BE DARING AND EXERCISE WHILE THE VEHICLE IS IN MOTION. SUDDEN STOPS MAY BE A THRILLING EXPERIENCE FOR A PERSON HANGING FROM THE *EXERCISE ROLL BAR*.

A. POSITION FOR COMMENCING TO USE *EXERCISE ROLL BAR*. STAND ON HEADRESTS, PLACING LEGS IN FRONT OF PADDED LEG-HOLDER. LEAN FORWARD, GRABBING LITTLE HANDLES, IF NECESSARY.

B. ONE OF THE MANY EXERCISES THAT CAN BE PERFORMED ON THE *EXERCISE ROLL BAR*.

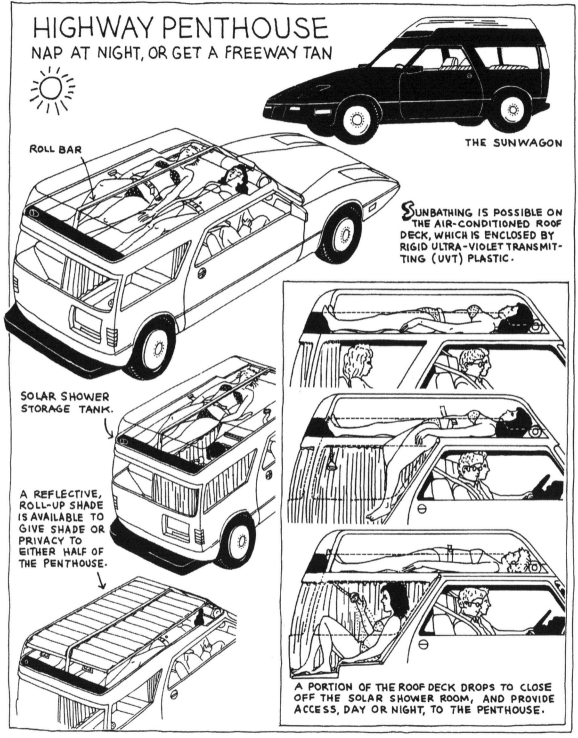

HIGHWAY PENTHOUSE
NAP AT NIGHT, OR GET A FREEWAY TAN

THE SUNWAGON

ROLL BAR

SUNBATHING IS POSSIBLE ON THE AIR-CONDITIONED ROOF DECK, WHICH IS ENCLOSED BY RIGID ULTRA-VIOLET TRANSMITTING (UVT) PLASTIC.

SOLAR SHOWER STORAGE TANK.

A REFLECTIVE, ROLL-UP SHADE IS AVAILABLE TO GIVE SHADE OR PRIVACY TO EITHER HALF OF THE PENTHOUSE.

A PORTION OF THE ROOF DECK DROPS TO CLOSE OFF THE SOLAR SHOWER ROOM, AND PROVIDE ACCESS, DAY OR NIGHT, TO THE PENTHOUSE.

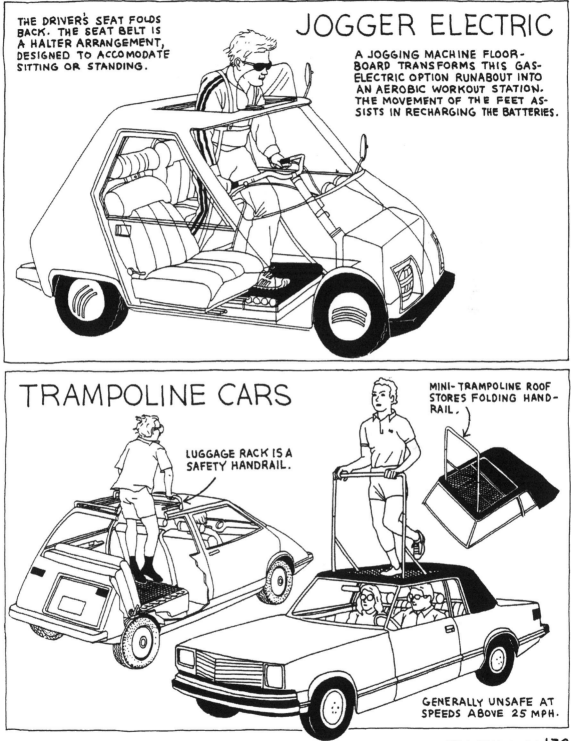

THE DRIVER'S SEAT FOLDS BACK. THE SEAT BELT IS A HALTER ARRANGEMENT, DESIGNED TO ACCOMODATE SITTING OR STANDING.

JOGGER ELECTRIC

A JOGGING MACHINE FLOORBOARD TRANSFORMS THIS GASELECTRIC OPTION RUNABOUT INTO AN AEROBIC WORKOUT STATION. THE MOVEMENT OF THE FEET ASSISTS IN RECHARGING THE BATTERIES.

TRAMPOLINE CARS

MINI-TRAMPOLINE ROOF STORES FOLDING HANDRAIL.

LUGGAGE RACK IS A SAFETY HANDRAIL.

GENERALLY UNSAFE AT SPEEDS ABOVE 25 MPH.

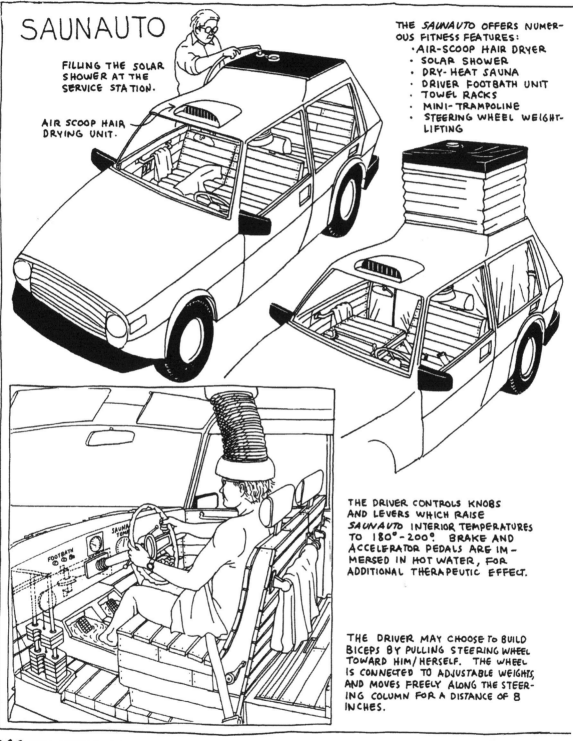

SAUNAUTO

FILLING THE SOLAR SHOWER AT THE SERVICE STATION.

AIR SCOOP HAIR DRYING UNIT.

THE *SAUNAUTO* OFFERS NUMEROUS FITNESS FEATURES:
- AIR-SCOOP HAIR DRYER
- SOLAR SHOWER
- DRY-HEAT SAUNA
- DRIVER FOOTBATH UNIT
- TOWEL RACKS
- MINI-TRAMPOLINE
- STEERING WHEEL WEIGHT-LIFTING

THE DRIVER CONTROLS KNOBS AND LEVERS WHICH RAISE *SAUNAUTO* INTERIOR TEMPERATURES TO 180°-200°. BRAKE AND ACCELERATOR PEDALS ARE IMMERSED IN HOT WATER, FOR ADDITIONAL THERAPEUTIC EFFECT.

THE DRIVER MAY CHOOSE TO BUILD BICEPS BY PULLING STEERING WHEEL TOWARD HIM/HERSELF. THE WHEEL IS CONNECTED TO ADJUSTABLE WEIGHTS, AND MOVES FREELY ALONG THE STEERING COLUMN FOR A DISTANCE OF 8 INCHES.

DURING TRIPS, PASSENGERS
AND DRIVER MAY ENJOY USING
THE SAUNA, WHILE SEATED ON
CEDAR BENCHES.

FOR ADDITIONAL EXERCISE, THE
SEATS MAY BE PULLED BACK
TO EXPOSE THE MINI-TRAMPOLINE.
TO JUMP OR JOG, THE ROOF
MUST BE RAISED.

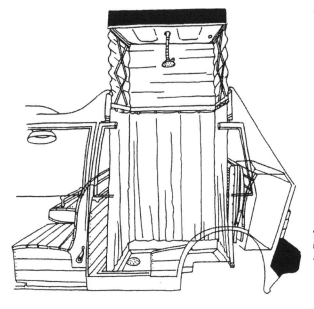

TO SHOWER, THE MINI-TRAMPOLINE
IS FOLDED BACK AND SHOWER CUR-
TAINS ARE LOWERED. BAFFLES
BENEATH THE SURFACE OF THE
SOLAR SHOWER MAY BE OPERATED
BY DRIVER, TO CONTROL SHOWER
HEAT. WHEN FULLY CLOSED, THE
SHOWER WATER WILL BE RELAT-
IVELY COLD, AS IS APPROPRIATE
AFTER A SAUNA BATH.

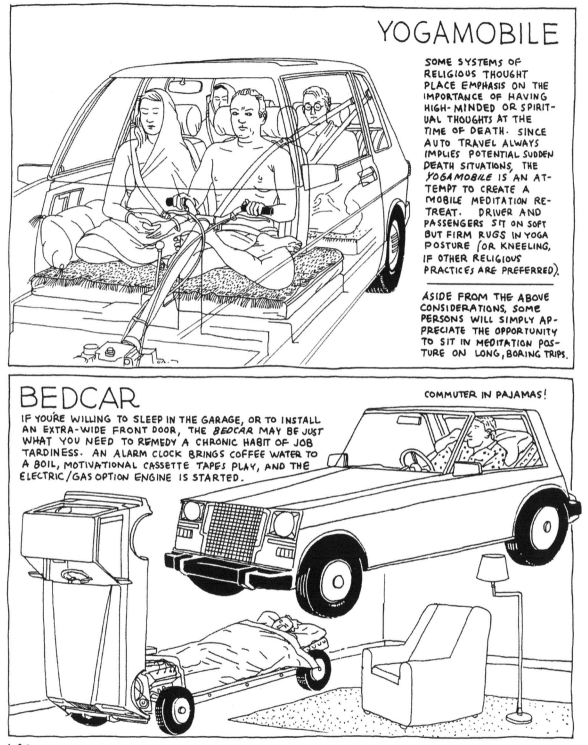

YOGAMOBILE

SOME SYSTEMS OF RELIGIOUS THOUGHT PLACE EMPHASIS ON THE IMPORTANCE OF HAVING HIGH-MINDED OR SPIRITUAL THOUGHTS AT THE TIME OF DEATH. SINCE AUTO TRAVEL ALWAYS IMPLIES POTENTIAL SUDDEN DEATH SITUATIONS, THE *YOGAMOBILE* IS AN ATTEMPT TO CREATE A MOBILE MEDITATION RETREAT. DRIVER AND PASSENGERS SIT ON SOFT BUT FIRM RUGS IN YOGA POSTURE (OR KNEELING, IF OTHER RELIGIOUS PRACTICES ARE PREFERRED).

ASIDE FROM THE ABOVE CONSIDERATIONS, SOME PERSONS WILL SIMPLY APPRECIATE THE OPPORTUNITY TO SIT IN MEDITATION POSTURE ON LONG, BORING TRIPS.

BEDCAR

COMMUTER IN PAJAMAS!

IF YOU'RE WILLING TO SLEEP IN THE GARAGE, OR TO INSTALL AN EXTRA-WIDE FRONT DOOR, THE *BEDCAR* MAY BE JUST WHAT YOU NEED TO REMEDY A CHRONIC HABIT OF JOB TARDINESS. AN ALARM CLOCK BRINGS COFFEE WATER TO A BOIL, MOTIVATIONAL CASSETTE TAPES PLAY, AND THE ELECTRIC/GAS OPTION ENGINE IS STARTED.

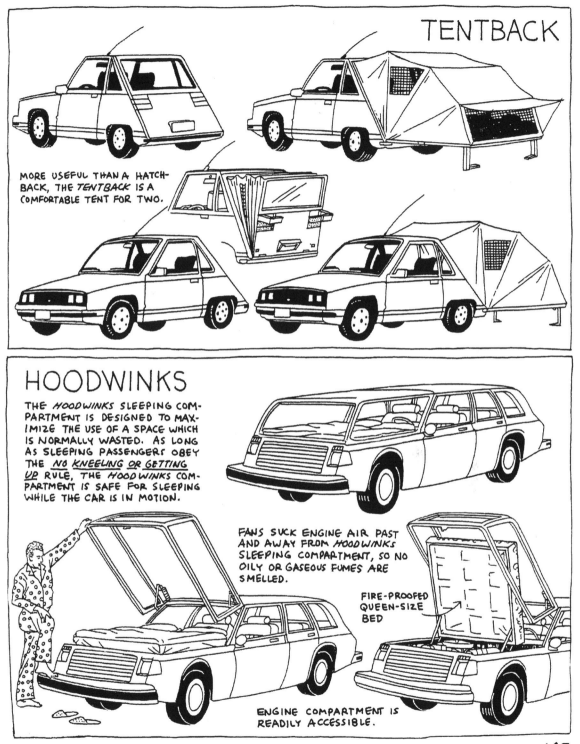

TENTBACK

MORE USEFUL THAN A HATCH-
BACK, THE *TENTBACK* IS A
COMFORTABLE TENT FOR TWO.

HOODWINKS

THE *HOODWINKS* SLEEPING COM-
PARTMENT IS DESIGNED TO MAX-
IMIZE THE USE OF A SPACE WHICH
IS NORMALLY WASTED. AS LONG
AS SLEEPING PASSENGERS OBEY
THE *NO KNEELING OR GETTING
UP* RULE, THE *HOODWINKS* COM-
PARTMENT IS SAFE FOR SLEEPING
WHILE THE CAR IS IN MOTION.

FANS SUCK ENGINE AIR PAST
AND AWAY FROM *HOODWINKS*
SLEEPING COMPARTMENT, SO NO
OILY OR GASEOUS FUMES ARE
SMELLED.

FIRE-PROOFED
QUEEN-SIZE
BED

ENGINE COMPARTMENT IS
READILY ACCESSIBLE.

BOATOMOBILE

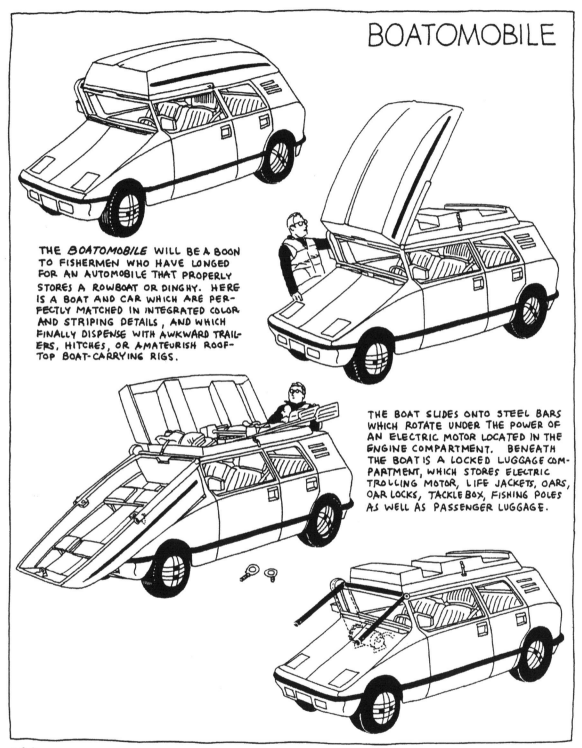

THE *BOATOMOBILE* WILL BE A BOON TO FISHERMEN WHO HAVE LONGED FOR AN AUTOMOBILE THAT PROPERLY STORES A ROWBOAT OR DINGHY. HERE IS A BOAT AND CAR WHICH ARE PERFECTLY MATCHED IN INTEGRATED COLOR AND STRIPING DETAILS, AND WHICH FINALLY DISPENSE WITH AWKWARD TRAILERS, HITCHES, OR AMATEURISH ROOFTOP BOAT-CARRYING RIGS.

THE BOAT SLIDES ONTO STEEL BARS WHICH ROTATE UNDER THE POWER OF AN ELECTRIC MOTOR LOCATED IN THE ENGINE COMPARTMENT. BENEATH THE BOAT IS A LOCKED LUGGAGE COMPARTMENT, WHICH STORES ELECTRIC TROLLING MOTOR, LIFE JACKETS, OARS, OAR LOCKS, TACKLE BOX, FISHING POLES AS WELL AS PASSENGER LUGGAGE.

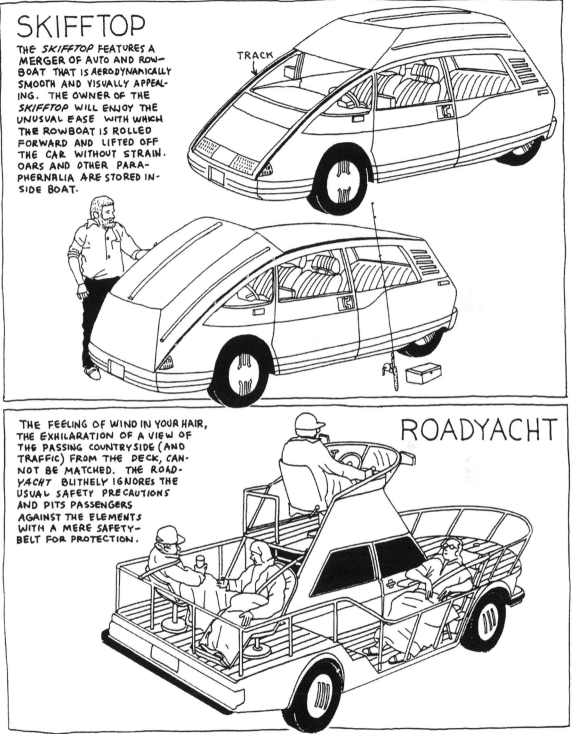

SKIFFTOP

THE *SKIFFTOP* FEATURES A MERGER OF AUTO AND ROW-BOAT THAT IS AERODYNAMICALLY SMOOTH AND VISUALLY APPEALING. THE OWNER OF THE *SKIFFTOP* WILL ENJOY THE UNUSUAL EASE WITH WHICH THE ROWBOAT IS ROLLED FORWARD AND LIFTED OFF THE CAR WITHOUT STRAIN. OARS AND OTHER PARAPHERNALIA ARE STORED INSIDE BOAT.

TRACK

ROADYACHT

THE FEELING OF WIND IN YOUR HAIR, THE EXHILARATION OF A VIEW OF THE PASSING COUNTRYSIDE (AND TRAFFIC) FROM THE DECK, CANNOT BE MATCHED. THE ROADYACHT BLITHELY IGNORES THE USUAL SAFETY PRECAUTIONS AND PITS PASSENGERS AGAINST THE ELEMENTS WITH A MERE SAFETYBELT FOR PROTECTION.

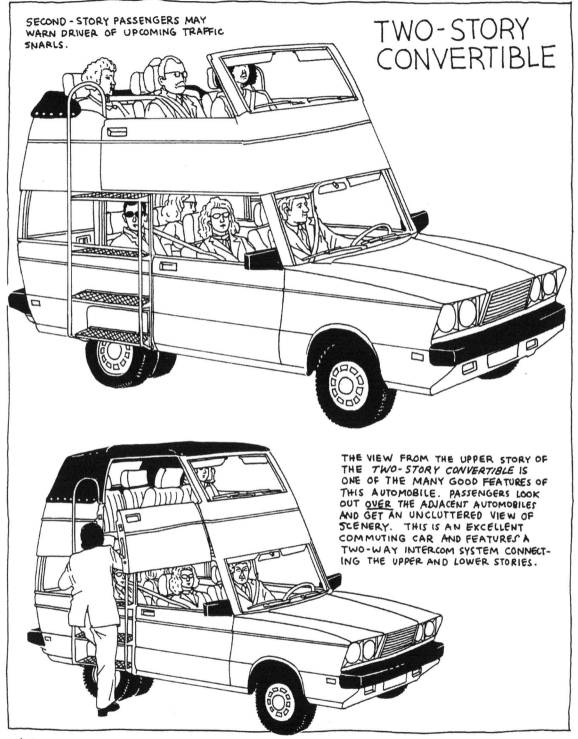

SECOND-STORY PASSENGERS MAY WARN DRIVER OF UPCOMING TRAFFIC SNARLS.

TWO-STORY CONVERTIBLE

THE VIEW FROM THE UPPER STORY OF THE *TWO-STORY CONVERTIBLE* IS ONE OF THE MANY GOOD FEATURES OF THIS AUTOMOBILE. PASSENGERS LOOK OUT OVER THE ADJACENT AUTOMOBILES AND GET AN UNCLUTTERED VIEW OF SCENERY. THIS IS AN EXCELLENT COMMUTING CAR AND FEATURES A TWO-WAY INTERCOM SYSTEM CONNECTING THE UPPER AND LOWER STORIES.

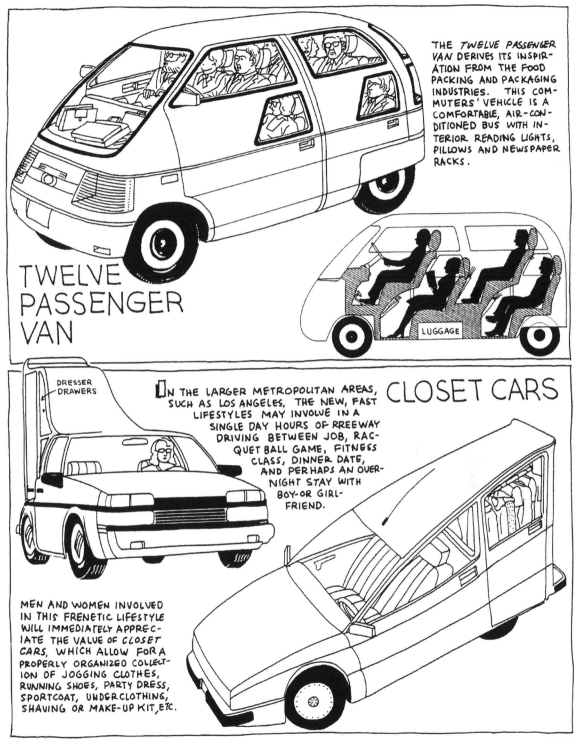

TWELVE PASSENGER VAN

THE *TWELVE PASSENGER VAN* DERIVES ITS INSPIR-ATION FROM THE FOOD PACKING AND PACKAGING INDUSTRIES. THIS COM-MUTERS' VEHICLE IS A COMFORTABLE, AIR-CON-DITIONED BUS WITH IN-TERIOR READING LIGHTS, PILLOWS AND NEWSPAPER RACKS.

LUGGAGE

DRESSER DRAWERS

CLOSET CARS

IN THE LARGER METROPOLITAN AREAS, SUCH AS LOS ANGELES, THE NEW, FAST LIFESTYLES MAY INVOLVE IN A SINGLE DAY HOURS OF FREEWAY DRIVING BETWEEN JOB, RAC-QUET BALL GAME, FITNESS CLASS, DINNER DATE, AND PERHAPS AN OVER-NIGHT STAY WITH BOY- OR GIRL-FRIEND.

MEN AND WOMEN INVOLVED IN THIS FRENETIC LIFESTYLE WILL IMMEDIATELY APPREC-IATE THE VALUE OF *CLOSET CARS*, WHICH ALLOW FOR A PROPERLY ORGANIZED COLLECT-ION OF JOGGING CLOTHES, RUNNING SHOES, PARTY DRESS, SPORTCOAT, UNDERCLOTHING, SHAVING OR MAKE-UP KIT, ETC.

ABNORMAL AUTOS

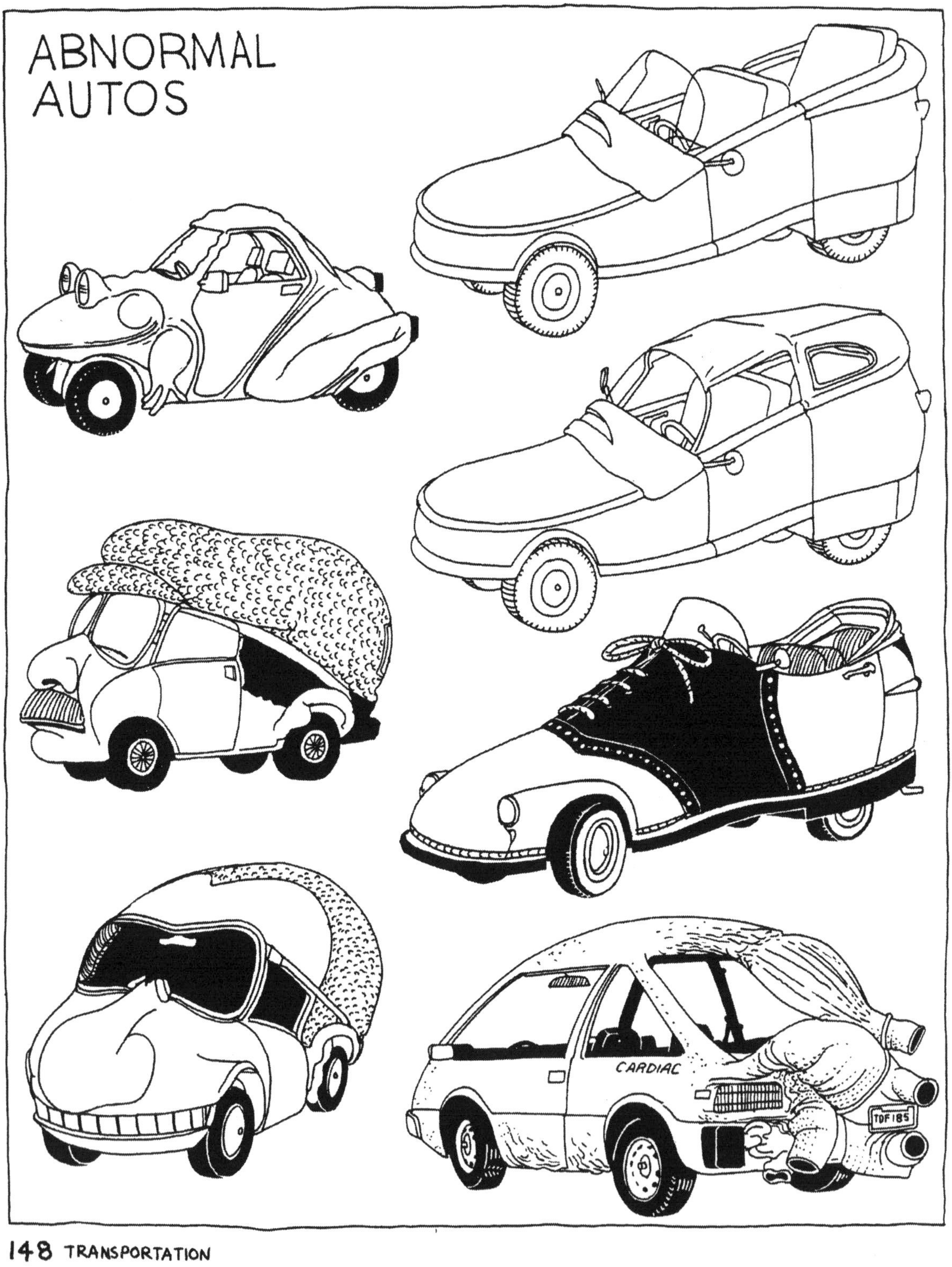
CARDIAC
TDF185

AUTHOR'S TIPS FOR INVENTING
USEFUL AND USELESS THINGS

I have developed a pattern that I follow when I wish to imagine new inventions. I sit on the living room rug at home and look out the window at the garden. I prefer to think up new concepts while I'm still sleepy in the morning. I avoid my desk and drafting table, as such furniture has the connotations of serious endeavor, deadlines, the real world, being responsible, and earning a living. I wish, instead, to be irresponsible, rash, associative, dreamy, impish, brainy, intuitive, and stupid.

THE FIRST STEP

Gathering up a stack of typing paper and a pen or pencil, I place these items on the floor beside me and look out the window. I find that a few key words and a blurry scribble are all that I need for capturing an idea, but it is important to note down all ideas, Like dream images, these products of the imagination evaporate easily and are usually impossible to retrieve later. I pick a topic: automobile bumpers. I focus my thoughts on existing styles of bumpers and begin to intentionally speed up my thinking process, causing a rapid succession of visual images to flash before my mind's eye. Thoughts are disjointed, associative, and sometimes humorous. I begin to stretch and condense images of fanciful bumpers in my mind as if they were made of clay.

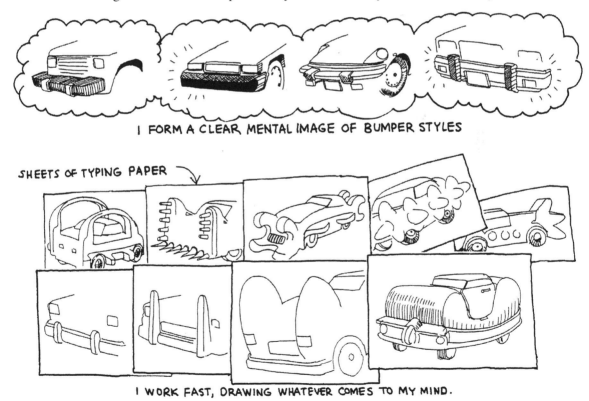

I FORM A CLEAR MENTAL IMAGE OF BUMPER STYLES

SHEETS OF TYPING PAPER

I WORK FAST, DRAWING WHATEVER COMES TO MY MIND.

HAMMER-HEAD

SABER-TOOTH

Buttresses

FILLED WITH SOMETHING SPONGY

BOXING GLOVE BUMPER

A HEAP OF DRAWINGS MAY ACCUMULATE ON THE LIVING ROOM RUG. I DRAW UNTIL I GET BORED OR TIRED.

MOST OF MY IDEAS AREN'T VERY PRACTICAL.

Now I have warmed up, and questions form rapidly: what is the history of the automobile bumper? I form images of old bumpers, historic bumpers, THE FIRST BUMPER, and things that were used formerly instead of bumpers. Did they evolve from some other invention? Why are they needed at all? I answer myself: to cushion from shock, to stand on, to be sacrificed so as to preserve the auto body, and to protect people. Why are there only front and rear bumpers, since some auto collisions involve oblique impact? At one time there were "running boards" along the sides of cars. I form the image of a WHOLE CAR BUMPER. This leads to a joke, THE WHOLE EARTH BUMPER, which I envision as a portable earthen berm, a rammed earth planter box, or a soil bumper. A bumper crop! At last, beginning to wake up, I have succeeded in amusing myself. An image forms of a car with a hedgerow, a freeway full of moving trees, cars with bushbumpers and foliage fenders. Then, questions form in my mind relating to pruning problems, driver visibility, damage to root systems from even minor bumps, and the weight of plant containers after a watering or heavy rain. I think of the complexity of auto insurance negotiations after damage caused by or to a bush. A few sketches are made, and I go on to other ideas. Finalizing things is not appropriate at this stage. I return to the WHOLE CAR BUMPER. What if cars looked like donuts and were encircled by rubber tire bumpers? I think of streets filled with donut cars and of a newspaper headline: LIVES SAVED BY DONUT CARS. I see cars gliding along slowly on slippery streets, massively padded, engaging in collisions just for fun! Now the concept of cars with soft, spongy or malleable surfaces is considered (and rejected).

The notion of flexible bumpers reminds me of water-filled bumper extenders with pop-out plugs which have been marketed. Thinking of these, I work on the idea of bumpers that squirt something, perhaps a fire retardant liquid; bumpers that squirt a noxious liquid, an evil-smelling substance, or perhaps something that spoils expensive paint finishes! Certainly such an invention would indirectly serve as a safety feature since vanity would make drivers cautious about hitting each other.

Moving along, I next ask myself to consider the things that cars usually hit: other cars, buildings, walls, trees, dogs, pedestrians. Pedestrians? Could there be bumpers which don't hurt or which are part of redesigned auto front ends, which would catch pedestrians in soft beds or nets? I ponder other things: bumpers that are accordions and play a tune when pressured, bumpers that hit back, either with pummeling arms or with an explosive charge that gives offending vehicles a sharp punch. I consider bumpers filled with sand, or bumpers that include pop-out air bags. By now I have generated dozens of nearly illegible notes which I save for future reference.

NOTES FOR PEDESTRIAN-CATCHING FRONT END.

THE SECOND STEP

At a later date, I review the stack of notes and consider which concepts are worth carrying to a further stage of elaboration. Does the idea work on any level, either as a gag, or as a real invention? Would the invention be structurally weak, dangerous, or is the idea better solved by other concepts?

THE THIRD STEP

I begin to prepare more detailed sketches of actual prototypes. This is a time-consuming process. I decide that I want to pursue the idea of planter box bumpers. Time may be spent researching various aspects of the idea: what kinds of bushes grow in shallow boxes, which plants are resistant to auto exhaust, when water is added how much does the water add to the weight of the car, and how deep can root systems go? I reach for a garden book, or go to the library. At this point I may abandon the idea and begin to develop another one. I decide to proceed, and roughly sketch alternative planter box bumpers.

THESE "PLANTER BOX BUMPERS" ARE MORE CAREFULLY DETAILED.

I finalize the version that appeals to me.

HERE, A TREE-WELL DESIGN, WITH DIVIDED FRONT SEAT, CAUGHT MY FANCY, AND I PRO-CEEDED TO DRAW A BIT MORE PRECISELY.

SHARPER LINES

THREE WATER SYSTEMS ARE PROVIDED: ① RADIATOR, ② WINDOW SQUIRTERS, AND ③ DRIP IRRIGATION OF PLANT-ER BUMPERS AND TREE WELL.

I have decided that the idea has no practical worth, and would never likely be adopted seriously (like most of my ideas), but I like it anyway. I can visualize a hypothetical suburban landscape with slow-moving vehicles like wheeled nurseries traversing beautiful, tree-lined avenues. I see roving greenhouses with plants inside and out. I see owner pride in horticultural excellence. Owners of autos, once willing to submit themselves and their loved ones to toxic levels of carbon monoxide and other poisonous fumes, rally to save their dying bumper plants. There is a sudden popular clamor to create electric and steam cars that are compatible with lovely tropical plants. New auto shapes evolve that provide advantageous configurations for planter beds.

This is the process I employ to imagine new inventions. The serious inventor would continue with mock-ups, materials tests, engineering drawings, patent applications and marketing strategy studies. But I am not a serious inventor.

Steven M. Johnson is a second-generation Californian, born in 1938 in San Rafael, California. He was educated at Yale University and the University of California at Berkeley. His whimsical product concepts first appeared in *The Sierra Club Bulletin* in 1974 and have since been published in numerous magazines including *Harper's, Road & Track, The Futurist, New Age Journal, Whole Earth Review, Nexus, Funny Times, Tur & Retur* (Sweden), *Box* (Japan), and *Brutus* (Japan). Since 2009 his work has appeared online in *The New York Times, The Atlantic, Good, FastCompany, Design Mind, Esquire* and *Txchnologist* as well as on other sites. *What The World Needs Now* appeared in 1984; in 1991, a subsequent collection of his drawings was published by St. Martin's Press *as Public Therapy Buses, Information Specialty Bums, Solar Cook-A-Mats and Other Visions of the 21st Century.* From 1989 to 1995, his work appeared weekly in *The Sacramento Bee* as "A Step Ahead," and was distributed from 1992-1995 by *Carmen Syndicate* as "Sightings." For a period of eight months from July, 2010 to March, 2011 his work appeared weekly *on www.neatorama.com* as "Museum of Possibilities."

He lives in California with his wife, Beatrice. His son, Alex, also lives in the state.

Made in the USA
San Bernardino, CA
18 April 2014